Mastering Backbone.js

Design and build scalable web applications using Backbone.js

Abiee Echamea

[PACKT] open source*
PUBLISHING   community experience distilled

BIRMINGHAM - MUMBAI

Mastering Backbone.js

First published: January 2016

Production reference: 1080116

Published by Packt Publishing Ltd.
Livery Place
35 Livery Street
Birmingham B3 2PB, UK.

ISBN 978-1-78328-849-6

www.packtpub.com

Credits

Author
Abiee Echamea

Reviewers
Mudassir Ali
Aleksandar Goševski
Lorenzo Pisani

Commissioning Editor
Rebika Yuvi

Acquisition Editor
Llewellyn Rozario

Content Development Editor
Susmita Sabat

Technical Editor
Danish Shaikh

Copy Editor
Vibha Shukla

Project Coordinator
Milton Dsouza

Proofreader
Safis Editing

Indexer
Hemangini Bari

Graphics
Disha Haria

Production Coordinator
Arvindkumar Gupta

Cover Work
Arvindkumar Gupta

About the Author

Abiee Echamea is a passionate technology software engineer; he fell in love with computers at the age of 8 and wrote his first program at 12. He has written applications in many technologies, from Visual Basic to full stack web applications. Now, Abiee is a software architect involved in the full development cycle, creating many Backbone applications successfully and designing the architecture and development process. He has founded a company to work with cutting-edge technology as a CTO. He has developed the skills to master the JavaScript and Backbone libraries to build maintainable projects for his company. Abiee loves to share his knowledge with the community and is looking for ways to improve his engineering skills.

About the Reviewers

Mudassir Ali is a senior frontend engineer at DiligenceVault. After working as a full stack web developer for a year and a half, he decided to specialize in frontend technologies due to his passion for the development of amazing user experiences by building effective user interfaces. In his three years of web development experience, he has worked on three major popular JavaScript frameworks: BackboneJS, AngularJS, and EmberJS. Besides his interest in frontend JavaScript and HTML5 technologies, he is also interested in designing JSON Apis using Ruby on Rails. He is also a regular contributor to the StackOverflow community and occasionally contributes to open source.

Aleksandar Goševski is a frontend engineer based in Belgrade, Serbia. He is a 23-year old senior developer with experience in creating websites and apps. He started with CSS but always wanted to do something more. As most of his work is focused for the web, his language of choice was JavaScript. Today, he uses JavaScript on both server side and client side. He is very passionate about Backbone and that's his favorite framework. Aleksandar is currently working for Vast.com. He is creating big single-page apps for clients mostly from USA. Coca-Cola, Allianz, Yahoo, Carfax, Bing, and AOL are just some of the big projects that Aleksandar has worked on.

Lorenzo Pisani is a software engineer with over a decade of experience developing applications with a large variety of languages and tools. As he slowly transitions to the land of DevOps, he hopes to help educate developers on how to best plan for their applications being deployed to production environments. As a huge advocate of open source software, he contributes everything that he builds, outside of work, to his GitHub profile (`https://github.com/Zeelot`) for others to use and learn from.

www.PacktPub.com

Support files, eBooks, discount offers, and more

For support files and downloads related to your book, please visit www.PacktPub.com.

Did you know that Packt offers eBook versions of every book published, with PDF and ePub files available? You can upgrade to the eBook version at www.PacktPub.com and as a print book customer, you are entitled to a discount on the eBook copy. Get in touch with us at service@packtpub.com for more details.

At www.PacktPub.com, you can also read a collection of free technical articles, sign up for a range of free newsletters and receive exclusive discounts and offers on Packt books and eBooks.

https://www2.packtpub.com/books/subscription/packtlib

Do you need instant solutions to your IT questions? PacktLib is Packt's online digital book library. Here, you can search, access, and readPackt's entire library of books.

Why subscribe?

- Fully searchable across every book published by Packt
- Copy and paste, print, and bookmark content
- On demand and accessible via a web browser

Free access for Packt account holders

If you have an account with Packt atwww.PacktPub.com, you can use this to access PacktLib today and view 9 entirely free books. Simply use your login credentials for immediate access.

Table of Contents

Preface

Backbone is an amazing library to build web applications; it's small, simple, and yet powerful. It provides a set of small and focused objects to be used as bricks when building frontend applications.

The beauty of Backbone is that it gives you the freedom to build your applications with your rules. However, with great power comes great responsibility; Backbone does not tell you anything about how to structure your applications. Keep in mind that Backbone is not a framework but a library.

After years of working with Backbone projects, making code experiments, and exploring code from other developers, I have identified patterns and best practices when building frontend web apps with Backbone.

This book explains how to give structure to your applications. It gives you the tools and strategies to create robust and maintainable web apps. It will help you define and assign the right responsibilities to the Backbone objects and define a new set of glue objects.

In the book, you will build a functional application applying the concepts that are exposed here. The application is simple enough to put in to practice the core concepts when building scalable frontend applications with Backbone. At any time, you can see the project code in the book repository at `https://github.com/abiee/mastering-backbone`.

What this book covers

Chapter 1, *Architecture of a Backbone application*, deals with the project organization at two levels: logical and physical. On the logical side, you will learn how to connect the Backbone objects, while on the physical side, you will see where to put your scripts.

Chapter 2, Managing views, helps you extract the common patterns of views and create a new set of general purpose views that can be used on any Backbone application. These views will remove a lot of boilerplate code when managing views.

Chapter 3, Model bindings, explains how to deal with complex REST resources and helps you handle embedded resources and keep it in sync with views.

Chapter 4, Modular code, covers dependency management and script bundling with Browserify. Modern applications are becoming more JavaScript-intensive, so it's a good idea to handle dependencies in a smarter way.

Chapter 5, Dealing with files, it covers the common requirement for web applications to upload files to a server, this chapter tells you how to do it in Backbone with a REST server.

Chapter 6, Store data in the browser, shows you how to store data in the browser and how to do it from a Backbone perspective. The chapter shows how to build two drivers to transparently store Backbone models in localStorage and indexedDB instead of a remote server. This can be useful if you want to create offline applications.

Chapter 7, Build like a pro, tells you how you can automatize common and repetitive tasks in a script. It will dramatically improve your productivity. It describes how you can build a development workflow that automatically refreshes your project every time you make a small change.

Chapter 8, Testing Backbone applications, shows you the strategies and best practices when testing frontend code.

Chapter 9, Deploy to production, shows you how to deploy the project to a production server. While high-demand applications need a sophisticated platform, this chapter gives you the starting point for small apps.

Chapter 10, Security, teaches you how to authenticate against the REST servers and how to manage sessions from the Backbone side.

What you need for this book

Though this book is for frontend applications, you will need to install Node version 5 or superior. Node will run the example REST server, automatize common tasks, and manage project dependencies.

Who this book is for

This book is made for developers who already know Backbone but want to create better projects; it does not explain Backbone from scratch. Instead, I will show you how to improve your skills to organize and structure your application in an effective way.

Conventions

In this book, you will find a number of text styles that distinguish between different kinds of information. Here are some examples of these styles and an explanation of their meaning.

Code words in text, database table names, folder names, filenames, file extensions, pathnames, dummy URLs, user input, and Twitter handles are shown as follows: "We can include other contexts through the use of the `include` directive."

A block of code is set as follows:

```
[default]
exten => s,1,Dial(Zap/1|30)
exten => s,2,Voicemail(u100)
exten => s,102,Voicemail(b100)
exten => i,1,Voicemail(s0)
```

When we wish to draw your attention to a particular part of a code block, the relevant lines or items are set in bold:

```
[default]
exten => s,1,Dial(Zap/1|30)
exten => s,2,Voicemail(u100)
exten => s,102,Voicemail(b100)
exten => i,1,Voicemail(s0)
```

Any command-line input or output is written as follows:

```
# cp /usr/src/asterisk-addons/configs/cdr_mysql.conf.sample
    /etc/asterisk/cdr_mysql.conf
```

New terms and important words are shown in bold. Words that you see on the screen, for example, in menus or dialog boxes, appear in the text like this: "Clicking the **Next** button moves you to the next screen."

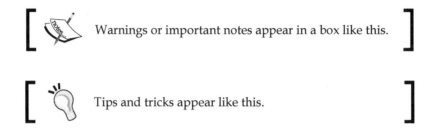

Warnings or important notes appear in a box like this.

Tips and tricks appear like this.

Reader feedback

Feedback from our readers is always welcome. Let us know what you think about this book—what you liked or disliked. Reader feedback is important for us as it helps us develop titles that you will really get the most out of.

To send us general feedback, simply e-mail feedback@packtpub.com, and mention the book's title in the subject of your message.

If there is a topic that you have expertise in and you are interested in either writing or contributing to a book, see our author guide at www.packtpub.com/authors.

Customer support

Now that you are the proud owner of a Packt book, we have a number of things to help you to get the most from your purchase.

Downloading the example code

You can download the example code files from your account at http://www.packtpub.com for all the Packt Publishing books you have purchased. If you purchased this book elsewhere, you can visit http://www.packtpub.com/support and register to have the files e-mailed directly to you.

Errata

Although we have taken every care to ensure the accuracy of our content, mistakes do happen. If you find a mistake in one of our books—maybe a mistake in the text or the code—we would be grateful if you could report this to us. By doing so, you can save other readers from frustration and help us improve subsequent versions of this book. If you find any errata, please report them by visiting http://www.packtpub.com/submit-errata, selecting your book, clicking on the **Errata Submission Form** link, and entering the details of your errata. Once your errata are verified, your submission will be accepted and the errata will be uploaded to our website or added to any list of existing errata under the Errata section of that title.

To view the previously submitted errata, go to https://www.packtpub.com/books/content/support and enter the name of the book in the search field. The required information will appear under the **Errata** section.

Piracy

Piracy of copyrighted material on the Internet is an ongoing problem across all media. At Packt, we take the protection of our copyright and licenses very seriously. If you come across any illegal copies of our works in any form on the Internet, please provide us with the location address or website name immediately so that we can pursue a remedy.

Please contact us at copyright@packtpub.com with a link to the suspected pirated material.

We appreciate your help in protecting our authors and our ability to bring you valuable content.

Questions

If you have a problem with any aspect of this book, you can contact us at questions@packtpub.com, and we will do our best to address the problem.

1
Architecture of a Backbone application

One of the best things about Backbone is the freedom to build applications with the libraries of your choice, no batteries included. Note that Backbone is not a framework but a library; due to this, building applications with Backbone can be challenging as no structure is provided. You, as a developer, are responsible for code organization and how to wire the pieces of the code across the application; it's a big responsibility. Bad decisions can lead to buggy and unmaintainable applications that nobody wants to work with.

Code organization on small Backbone applications is not a big deal. Create a directory for models, collections, and views; put a router for all possible routes; and write the business logic directly in the views. However, this way of developing Backbone applications is not suitable for bigger projects. There should be a better way to separate responsibilities and file organization in order to create maintainable applications.

This chapter can be difficult to understand if you don't know Backbone at all; to understand the principles that are exposed here better, you will need to understand at least the basics of Backbone. Therefore, if you are a beginner in Backbone, I would encourage you to first understand what Backbone is and how it works.

The goal of this chapter is to explore the best practices of project organization on two main levels: logic organization and file structure. In this chapter, you will learn the following:

- Delegating the right responsibilities to the objects provided by Backbone
- Defining plain JavaScript objects in order to deal with logic out of scope of Backbone objects
- Splitting the application in to small and maintainable scripts
- Creating a clean file structure for your projects

Subapplications based architecture

We can compose a Backbone application with many independent subapplications. The subapplications should work independently. You can think about each one as a small Backbone application, with its own dependencies and responsibilities; it should not depend on other subapplications directly.

Subapplications should be focused on a specific domain area. For example, you can have a subapplication for invoices, another for the mailbox, and one more for payments; with these subapplications in place, you can build an application in order to manage payments through email.

To decouple subapplications from each other, we can build an infrastructure application responsible for managing the subapplications, bootstrapping the whole application, and providing the subapplications with common functions and services:

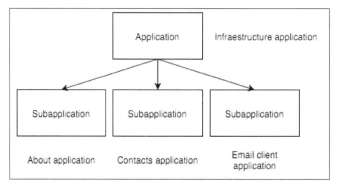

Figure 1.1. Composition of a Backbone application with subapplications

You can use the infrastructure application to provide your subapplications with services such as confirmation and dialog messages, notification pop-ups, modal boxes, and so on. The infrastructure application does nothing by itself, it behaves as a framework for the subapplications.

When a subapplication wants to communicate with another subapplication, the infrastructure application can be used as a communication channel, it can take advantage of the `Backbone.Event` object in order to send and receive messages.

In the following figure, you can see a scenario where the subapplications communicate through the infrastructure application. When the user clicks on **Compose message** in the Mailbox subapplication, the infrastructure application creates and renders the **Compose mail** subapplication and allows the user to write an e-mail.

When the user is done, they have to click on the **Send** button in the **Compose** subapplication; then the e-mail is sent through a RESTful API or using plain SMTP, don't care, the important thing is that, when it finishes, it triggers an event in the email:sent infrastructure application.

The infrastructure application forwards the event to the Mailbox subapplication, so that the list of emails that are sent can be updated. Another interesting thing is that the infrastructure application can use the email:sent event to show a successful pop-up message to the user to tell them that the email was successfully sent:

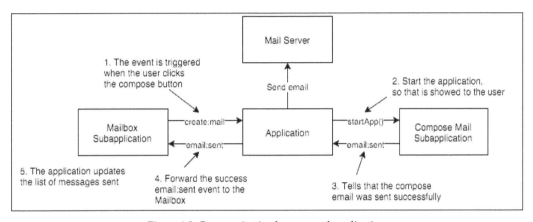

Figure 1.2. Communication between subapplications

Subapplication anatomy

As mentioned earlier, a subapplication is like a small Backbone application; they should be independent of other subapplications and work as a standalone. You should be able to put the Compose mail subapplication on a blank page without any other subapplication and still be able to send emails.

To achieve this, the subapplications should contain all the necessary objects that are to be auto-contained. You can see that the entry point of the subapplication is Backbone.Router. When the browser changes the URL and a route is matched for a given subapplication, the router creates a subapplication controller and delegates it the route handling.

The subapplication controller coordinates the models/collections and how they are shown. The controller can instruct the **Application** infrastructure to show a loading message while the data is fetched and when it's done, the controller can build the necessary views with the models and collections that are recently fetched in order to show them in the DOM.

In short, a subapplication behaves exactly like a small Backbone application, with the main difference being that it uses the Application infrastructure to delegate common tasks and a communication channel between the subapplications.

In the next sections, we will examine how these parts are connected and I will show you the code for a working Contacts application. The following figure shows an anatomy view of a subapplication:

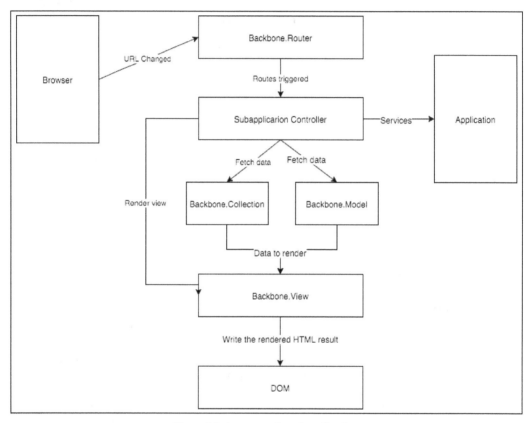

Figure 1.3. Anatomy of a subapplication

Responsibilities of Backbone objects

One of the biggest issues with the Backbone documentation is not to have a clue about how to use its objects. You, as developers, should figure out the responsibilities for each object across the application; if you have some experience working with Backbone, then you would know how difficult it would be to build a Backbone application.

In this section, I will describe the best uses of the Backbone objects. Starting at this point, you will have a clearer idea about the scope of responsibilities in Backbone and this will lead the design of our application architecture. Keep in mind that Backbone is a library with only the foundation objects; therefore, you will need to bring your own objects and structure to make scalable, testable, and robust Backbone applications.

Views

The only responsibilities of views are to handle the **Document Object Model** (**DOM**) and listen for low-level events (jQuery/DOM events), and transform them into domain ones. The Backbone Views works closely with template engines in order to create markups that represent the information that is contained in models and collections.

Views abstract the user interactions, transforming their actions into business value data structures for the application. For example, when a click event is triggered from a Save button in the DOM, the view should transform the event into something similar to a `save:contact` event using Backbone Events with the data written in the form. Then, a domain-specific object can apply some business logic to the data and show a result.

It is a rule that business logic on views should be avoided; however, basic form validations such as accept only numbers are allowed. Complex validations should still be done on the model or the controller.

Models

Backbone Models are like database gateways in the server side, their main use is to fetch and save data to and from a RESTful server and then provide an API to the rest of the application in order to handle the information. They can run general-purpose business logic, such as validation and data transformation, handle other server connections, and upload an image for a model.

The models do not know anything about views; however, they can implement functionality that is useful for views. For example, you can have a view that shows the total of an invoice and the invoice model can implement a method that does the calculation, leaving the view without knowledge of the computation.

Collections

You can think of Backbone Collections as a container of a set of Backbone Models, for example, a Collection of `Contacts` models. With a model, you can only fetch a single document at time; however, Collections allow us to fetch lists of Models.

A big difference from Models is that Collections should be used as read-only, they fetch the data but they should not write in the server; also it is not usual to see business logic here.

Another use for Collection is to abstract RESTful APIs responses as each server has different ways to deal with a list of resources. For instance, while some servers accept a `skip` parameter for pagination, others have a `page` parameter for the same purpose. Another case is on responses, a server can respond with a plain array, while others prefer to send an object with a `data`, `list`, or other key, where the array of objects is placed. There is no standard way. Collections can deal with these issues, making server requests transparent for the rest of the application.

Routers

Routers have a simple responsibility: listening for URL changes in the browser and transforming them into a call to a handler. A router knows which handler to call for a given URL. Also, they have to decode URL parameters and pass them to the handlers. The infrastructure application bootstraps the application; however, routers decide which subapplication will be executed. In this way, routers are a kind of entry point.

Objects not provided by Backbone

It is possible to develop Backbone applications only using the Backbone objects that are described in the previous section; however, for a medium-to-large application, it's not sufficient. We need to introduce a new kind of object with delimited responsibilities that use and coordinate Backbone foundation objects.

Subapplication façade

This object is the public interface of the subapplications. Any interaction with the subapplications should be done through its methods. The calls made directly to internal objects of the subapplication are discouraged. Typically, methods on this controller are called from the router; however, they can be called from anywhere.

The main responsibility of this object is to simplify subapplication internals. Its main work is to fetch data from the server through models or collections and, if an error occurs during the process, it is responsible to show an error message to the user. Once the data is loaded in a model or collection, it creates a subapplication controller that knows the views which should be rendered and have the handlers deal with its events.

Subapplication controller

A controller acts like an air traffic controller for views, models, and collections. When given a Backbone data object, it will instantiate and render the appropriate views and then coordinate them. On complex layouts, it is not an easy task to coordinate the views with the models and collections.

The Business logic for the use cases should be implemented here. The subapplication controller implements a **mediator pattern**, allowing other basic objects such as views and models keep it simple and loose coupling.

Due to loose coupling reasons, a view should not directly call to methods or events of other views Instead of this, a view triggers events and the controller handles the event and orchestrates the views behavior if necessary. Note how views are isolated, handling just its owned portion of DOM and triggering events when required to communicate something.

Contacts application

In this book, we will develop a simple contacts application in order to demonstrate how to develop Backbone applications following the principles explained throughout this book. The application should be able to list all the available contacts in RESTful API and provide the mechanisms to show and edit them.

The application starts when the Application infrastructure is loaded in the browser and the start() method on it is called. It will bootstrap all the common components and then instantiate all the available routers in the subapplications:

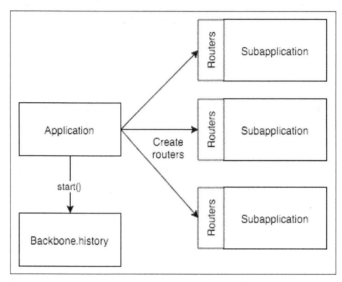

Figure 1.4. Application instantiates all the routers available in the subapplications

```
// app.js
var App = {
  Models: {},
  Collections: {},
  Routers: {},
  start() {
    // Initialize all available routes
    _.each(_.values(this.Routers), function(Router) {
      new Router();
    });

    // Create a global router to enable sub-applications to
    // redirect to other urls
    App.router = new DefaultRouter();
    Backbone.history.start();
  }
}
```

The entry point of subapplication is given by its routes, which ideally share the same namespace. For instance, in the contacts subapplication, all the routes start with the `contacts/` prefix:

- `Contacts`: This lists all available contacts
- `contacts/new`: This shows a form to create a new contact
- `contacts/view/:id`: This shows an invoice given its ID
- `contacts/edit/:id`: This shows a form to edit a contact

Subapplications should register its routers in the `App.Routers` global object in order to be initialized. For the Contacts subapplication, the `ContactsRouter` does the job:

```
// apps/contacts/router.js
'use strict';

App.Routers = App.Routers || {};

class ContactsRouter extends Backbone.Router {
  constructor(options) {
    super(options);
    this.routes = {
      'contacts': 'showContactList',
      'contacts/page/:page': 'showContactList',
      'contacts/new': 'createContact',
      'contacts/view/:id': 'showContact',
      'contacts/edit/:id': 'editContact'
    };
    this._bindRoutes();
  }

  showContactList(page) {
    // Page should be a postive number grater than 0
    page = page || 1;
    page = page > 0 ? page : 1;

    var app = this.startApp();
    app.showContactList(page);
  }

  createContact() {
    var app = this.startApp();
```

```
        app.showNewContactForm();
    }

    showContact(contactId) {
      var app = this.startApp();
      app.showContactById(contactId);
    }

    editContact(contactId) {
      var app = this.startApp();
      app.showContactEditorById(contactId);
    }

    startApp() {
      return App.startSubApplication(ContactsApp);
    }
  }

  // Register the router to be initialized by the infrastructure
  // Application
  App.Routers.ContactsRouter = ContactsRouter;
```

When the user points its browser to one of these routes, a route handler is triggered. The handler function parses the URL and delegates the request to the subapplication façade:

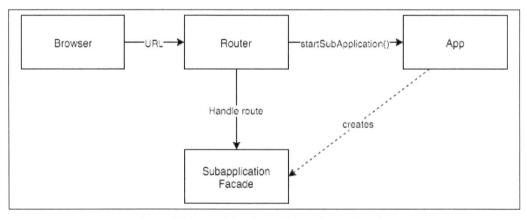

Figure 1.5. Route delegation to Subapplication Façade

The `startSubApplication()` method in the `App` object starts a new subapplication and closes any other subapplication that is running at a given time, this is useful to free resources in the user's browser:

```
var App = {
  // ...
  // Only a subapplication can be running at once, destroy any
  // current running subapplication and start the asked one
  startSubApplication(SubApplication) {
    // Do not run the same subapplication twice
    if (this.currentSubapp &&
        this.currentSubapp instanceof SubApplication) {
      return this.currentSubapp;
    }

    // Destroy any previous subapplication if we can
    if (this.currentSubapp && this.currentSubapp.destroy) {
      this.currentSubapp.destroy();
    }

    // Run subapplication
    this.currentSubapp = new SubApplication({
      region: App.mainRegion
    });
    return this.currentSubapp;
  },
}
```

> **Downloading the example code**
>
> You can download the example code files from your account at http://www.packtpub.com for all the Packt Publishing books you have purchased. If you purchased this book elsewhere, you can visit http://www.packtpub.com/support and register to have the files e-mailed directly to you.

The `App.mainRegion` attribute is an instance of a `Region` object that points to a DOM element in the page; regions are useful to render views in a contained region of the DOM. We will learn more about this object in *Chapter 2, Managing views.*

When the subapplication is started, a façade method is called on it to handle the user request. The responsibility of the façade is to fetch the necessary data from the RESTful API and pass the data to a controller:

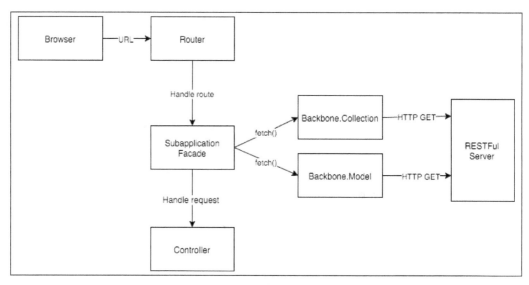

Figure 1.6. Façade responsibility

```javascript
// apps/contacts/app.js
'use strict';

class ContactsApp {
  constructor(options) {
    this.region = options.region;
  }

  showContactList() {
    App.trigger('loading:start');
    App.trigger('app:contacts:started');

    new ContactCollection().fetch({
      success: (collection) => {
        // Show the contact list subapplication if
        // the list can be fetched
        this.showList(collection);
        App.trigger('loading:stop');
      },
      fail: (collection, response) => {
        // Show error message if something goes wrong
        App.trigger('loading:stop');
```

```
        App.trigger('server:error', response);
      }
    });
  }

  showNewContactForm() {
    App.trigger('app:contacts:new:started');
    this.showEditor(new Contact());
  }

  showContactEditorById(contactId) {
    App.trigger('loading:start');
    App.trigger('app:contacts:started');

    new Contact({id: contactId}).fetch({
      success: (model) => {
        this.showEditor(model);
        App.trigger('loading:stop');
      },
      fail: (collection, response) => {
        App.trigger('loading:stop');
        App.trigger('server:error', response);
      }
    });
  }

  showContactById(contactId) {
    App.trigger('loading:start');
    App.trigger('app:contacts:started');

    new Contact({id: contactId}).fetch({
      success: (model) => {
        this.showViewer(model);
        App.trigger('loading:stop');
      },
      fail: (collection, response) => {
        App.trigger('loading:stop');
        App.trigger('server:error', response);
      }
    });
  }

  showList(contacts) {
    var contactList = this.startController(ContactList);
```

```
      contactList.showList(contacts);
    }

    showEditor(contact) {
      var contactEditor = this.startController(ContactEditor);
      contactEditor.showEditor(contact);
    }

    showViewer(contact) {
      var contactViewer = this.startController(ContactViewer);
      contactViewer.showContact(contact);
    }

    startController(Controller) {
      if (this.currentController &&
          this.currentController instanceof Controller) {
        return this.currentController;
      }

      if (this.currentController &&
          this.currentController.destroy) {
        this.currentController.destroy();
      }

      this.currentController = new Controller({
        region: this.region
      });
      return this.currentController;
    }
}
```

The façade object receives a region object as argument in order to indicate to the subapplication where it should be rendered. The Region objects will be explained in detail in *Chapter 2, Managing views*.

When the façade is fetching data from the RESTful server, a loading:start event is emitted on the App object in order to allow us to show the loading in progress view for the user. When the loading finishes, it creates and uses a controller that knows how to deal with the model or fetched collection.

The business logic starts when the controller is invoked, it will render all the necessary views for the request and show them to the user, then it will listen for user interactions in the views:

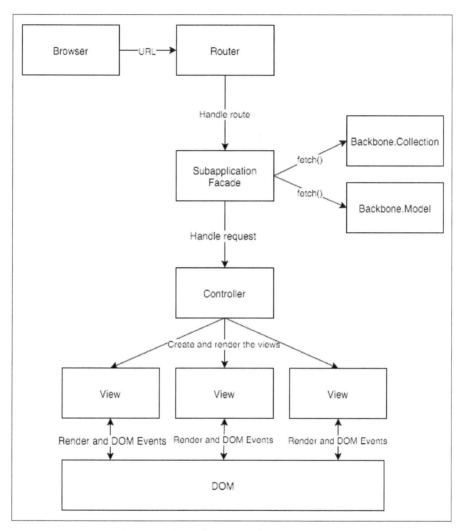

Figure 1.7. Controller creates the necessary views

For the ContactList controller, here is a very simple code:

```
// apps/contacts/contactLst.js
class ContactList {
  constructor(options) {
    // Region where the application will be placed
```

```
    this.region = options.region;

    // Allow subapplication to listen and trigger events,
    // useful for subapplication wide events
    _.extend(this, Backbone.Events);
}

showList(contacts) {
    // Create the views
    var layout = new ContactListLayout();
    var actionBar = new ContactListActionBar();
    var contactList = new ContactListView({collection: contacts});

    // Show the views
    this.region.show(layout);
    layout.getRegion('actions').show(actionBar);
    layout.getRegion('list').show(contactList);

    this.listenTo(contactList, 'item:contact:delete',
        this.deleteContact);
}

createContact() {
    App.router.navigate('contacts/new', true);
}

deleteContact(view, contact) {
    let message = 'The contact will be deleted';
    App.askConfirmation(message, (isConfirm) => {
        if (isConfirm) {
            contact.destroy({
                success() {
                    App.notifySuccess('Contact was deleted');
                },
                error() {
                    App.notifyError('Ooops... Something went wrong');
                }
            });
        }
    });
}

// Close any active view and remove event listeners
// to prevent zombie functions
```

```
destroy() {
  this.region.remove();
  this.stopListening();
}
}
```

The function that handles the request is very simple and follows the same pattern for all other controllers, as follows:

- It creates all the necessary views with the model or collection that is passed
- It renders the views in a region of the DOM
- It listens for events in the views

If you don't entirely understand what region and layout means, don't worry, I will cover the implementation of these objects in detail in *Chapter 2, Managing views*. Here, the important thing is the algorithm described earlier:

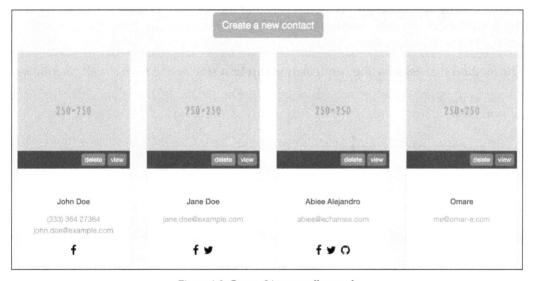

Figure 1.8. ContactList controller result

As you can see in the above figure, the contact list shows a set of cards for each contact in the list. The user is allowed to delete a contact by clicking on the **delete** button. When this happens, a `contact:delete` event is triggered, the controller is listening for the event and uses the `deleteContact()` method to handle the event:

```
deleteContact(view, contact) {
  let message = 'The contact will be deleted';
  App.askConfirmation(message, (isConfirm) => {
    if (isConfirm) {
```

```
      contact.destroy({
        success() {
          App.notifySuccess('Contact was deleted');
        },
        error() {
          App.notifyError('Ooops... Something went wrong');
        }
      });
    }
  });
}
```

The handler is pretty easy to understand, it uses the `askConfirmation()` method in the infrastructure app to ask for the user confirmation. If the user confirms the deletion, the contact is destroyed. The infrastructure App provides two methods to show notifications to the user: `notifySuccess()` and `notifyError()`.

The cool thing about these App methods is that the controllers do not need to know the details about the confirmation and notification mechanisms. From the controller point of view, it just works.

The method that asks for the confirmation can be a simple `confirm()` call, as follows:

```
// app.js
var App = {
  // ...
  askConfirmation(message, callback) {
    var isConfirm = confirm(message);
    callback(isConfirm);
  }
};
```

However, in the modern web applications, using the plain `confirm()` function is not the best way to ask for confirmation. Instead, we can show a Bootstrap dialog box or use an available library for that. For simplicity, we will use the nice JavaScript `SweetAlert` library; however, you can use whatever you want:

```
// app.js
var App = {
  // ...

  askConfirmation(message, callback) {
    var options = {
      title: 'Are you sure?',
      type: 'warning',
```

```
        text: message,
        showCancelButton: true,
        confirmButtonText: 'Yes, do it!',
        confirmButtonColor: '#5cb85c',
        cancelButtonText: 'No'
    };

    // Show the message
    swal(options, function(isConfirm) {
      callback(isConfirm);
    });
  }
};
```

Figure 1.9. Using SweetAlert for confirmation messages

We can implement the notification methods in a similar way. We will use the JavaScript `noty` library; however, you can use whatever you want:

```
// app.js
var App = {
  // ...

    notifySuccess(message) {
    new noty({
      text: message,
      layout: 'topRight',
      theme: 'relax',
      type: 'success',
      timeout: 3000 // close automatically
    });
```

```
    },

  notifyError(message) {
    new noty({
      text: message,
      layout: 'topRight',
      theme: 'relax',
      type: 'error',
      timeout: 3000 // close automatically
    });
  }
};
```

Figure 1.10. Using noty to show notification messages

This is how you can implement a robust and maintainable Backbone application; please go to the GitHub repo for this book in order to see the complete code for the application. The views are not covered in the chapter as we will see them in detail in *Chapter 2, Managing views*.

File organization

When you work with MVC frameworks, file organization is trivial. However, Backbone is not an MVC framework, therefore, bringing your own file structure is the rule. You can organize the code on these paths:

- apps/: This directory is where modules or subapplications live. All subapplications should be on this path
- Components/: These are the common components that multiple subapplications require or use on the common layout as a breadcrumbs component
- core/: Under this path, we can put all the core functions such as utilities, helpers, adapters, and so on
- vendor/: On vendor, you can put all third-party libraries; here you can put Backbone and its dependencies.
- app.js: This is the entry point of the application that is loaded from index.html

- Subapplications can have a file structure as they are a small Backbone Application.
- `models/`: This defines the models and collections
- `app.js`: This is the application façade that is called from the router
- `router.js`: This is the router of the application that is instantiated by the root application at bootstrap process
- `contactList.js`, `contactEditor.js`, `contactViewer.js`: These are the controllers for the application

For a `contacts` application, the code organization can be as shown in the following:

Figure 1.11. File structure

Summary

We started by describing, in a general way, how a Backbone application works. It describes two main parts: a root application and subapplications. The root application provides a common infrastructure to other smaller and focused applications that we call subapplications.

Subapplications should be loose coupled with other subapplications and should own its resources such as views, controllers, routers, and so on. A subapplication manages a small part of the system with a well-focused business value and the communication between subapplications and infrastructure application is made through an events-driven bus with `Backbone.Events`.

The user interacts with the application using views that a subapplication renders. A subapplication controller orchestrates interaction between views, models, and collections and owns the business logic for the use case.

Finally, a file system organization explains the right sites to put your files and keep your project clean and organized. This organization does not follow an MVC pattern; however, it is powerful and simple. It encapsulates all the necessary code for a module in a single path (subapplication paths) instead of putting all the code across multiple paths.

In this way the structure of Backbone applications has been proven to be robust, a proof for this is that several open source applications such as TodoMVC follow (more or less) the principles exposed here. It facilitates the testability of the code due to separation of responsibilities so that each object can be tested separately.

Large Backbone applications are often built on top of Backbone Marionette as it reduces the boilerplate code; however, Marionette uses its own conventions to work. If you are fine with it using its own conventions, you will be happy to use Marionette on top of Backbone.

However, if you love the freedom of doing things your way, you may prefer plain Backbone and create your own utilities and classes.

In the next chapter, I will show you how to manage and organize views and simplify the complex layouts, identifying the common uses of the views. You will build general purpose views that will be useful for all your projects and forget about the implementation of the `render()` method.

2
Managing Views

As we have seen in the previous chapter, Backbone views are responsible for managing **DOM (Document Object Model)** interactions between users and applications. A typical Backbone application is composed of many views with a very specific behavior; for instance, we can have a view to show contact data and another view to edit it. As you know, rendering a single view is a trivial task, but orchestrating a complex layout with multiple views can be a pain.

It's important to develop a better strategy to deal with complex view interactions to make the project easier to maintain and fun to develop. If you don't put the necessary attention into the organization of your views you can end up with a dirty DOM and messy code, which makes it hard to introduce new features or change existing ones.

As we did in the previous chapter, we are going to separate responsibilities by identifying common view use cases and then will learn how to compose layouts by using small views.

In this chapter you will learn to:

- Identify common view types
- Implement reusable views for common types
- Use the reusable view types to compose complex views easily

Identifying view types

After working with Backbone for a while you can see common use cases for views emerge; they are so common they can be used for different unrelated projects. These views can be extracted and can be used on any project if they are built correctly. Looking at the Backbone documentation, Views do not implement a default render method, so the trick here is to define a set of views with a default render method for different use cases:

- **View with model** – Render a template with model data.

- **View with collection** – Render a collection of views with collection data; it should update the list of views automatically when the collection changes.

- **Region** – This view acts like a container; it points to a particular DOM node and manages the content for that node. It's used to render other views.

- **Layout** – A layout is composed of one or more regions; it defines an HTML structure to organize where the regions will be placed.

Figure 2.1 shows a simple wireframe for an application; as you can see, it is a very common layout found on web applications and is very useful to understand how the common view types are related.

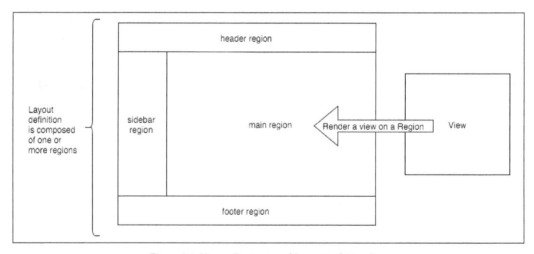

Figure 2.1: Views, Regions, and Layout relationship

With these foundation views you will have a simple but powerful framework to manage your views, so you won't need to implement the `render()` method anymore.

ModelView

The simplest implementation is to render a single model; it's a very straightforward algorithm. Extract data from the model and use a template engine to make the actual render with the data; finally, attach the result in the DOM:

```
class MyView extends Backbone.View {
  constructor(options) {
    super(options);
    template: _.template($("#my-template").html());
  }

  render() {
      var data = this.model.toJSON();
    var renderedHtml = this.template(data);
    this.$el.html(renderedHtml);
    return this;
  }
}
```

In the following code we can identify five steps to rendering the view.

1. Get the template:

    ```
    $("#my-template").html()
    ```

2. Compile the template:

    ```
    _.template($("#my-template").html())
    ```

3. Get data from the model:

    ```
    var data = this.model.toJSON()
    ```

4. Render the template with model data:

    ```
    renderedHtml = this.template(data)
    ```

5. Put the result on the DOM:

    ```
    this.$el.html(renderedHtml)
    ```

Note that we return this in the `render()` method; this is useful for chaining calls. These steps are common for all views that need to render a model, so we can extract that behavior in a new view type. This view will own the generic algorithm and let the specific parts open to extend:

```
class ModelView extends Backbone.View {
  render() {
    var data = this.serializeData();

    // Compile the template
    var renderedHtml = _.template(this.template, data);

    // Put the result in the DOM
    this.$el.html(renderedHtml);
    return this;
  }

  serializeData() {
    var data;

    // Serialize only if a model is present
    if (this.model) {
      data = this.model.toJSON();
    }

    return data;
  }
});
```

The model data now is done in a separated method, `serializeData()`, allowing us to implement a different way to provide data to the view; however, it implements a default behavior that is needed in most cases.

The template is now compiled in the process using the Underscore template engine, so that you have to provide the template text and let it make the rest. But this leaves the view highly coupled with a template engine; what if you need to use a different one such as Handlebars?

We can use the same strategy as before in the `serializedData()` method, and put this behavior in a separated method. All template engines need two things: template text and data. Template text can be obtained by a jQuery selector, a string variable, pre-compiled template, and so on. So we will leave this open to the final implementation:

```
class ModelView extends Backbone.View {
    // Compile template with underscore templates. This method
    // can be redefined to implemente another template engine
    // like Handlebars or Jade
    compileTemplate() {
      var $el = $(this.template);
      return _.template($el.html());
    }

    // ...
}
```

And, as we did with `serializedData()`, a default behavior is implemented.

```
class ModelView extends Backbone.View {
  render() {
    // Get JSON representation of the model
    var data = this.serializeData();
    var renderedHtml;

    // If template is a function assume that is a compiled
    // template, if not assume that is a CSS selector where
    // the template is defined and is compatible with
    // underscore templates
    if (_.isFunction(this.template)) {
      renderedHtml = this.template(data);
    } else if (_.isString(this.template)) {
      var compiledTemplate = this.compileTemplate();
      renderedHtml = compiledTemplate(data);
    }

    this.$el.html(renderedHtml);
    return this;
  }

  // ...
}
```

In this case, the `template` property can be either a function or a string. If a string is used, the default behavior will be to use the Underscore template engine. If a function is used, the function gives us the freedom to use any template engine.

If we want to render a model in a view, we can do something like this:

```
var contact = new Backbone.Model({
  name: 'John Doe',
  phone: '5555555'
});

var ContactView extends ModelView {
  constructor(options) {
    super(options);
    this.template = $('#contact-template').html();
  }

  // ... anything else like event handlers
}

var contactView = new ContactView({
  model: contact,
  el: 'body'
});
contactView.render();
```

You only need to specify the template and the model, and you're done!

CollectionView

Backbone Collections are composed of many models, so when rendering a collection what we need is to render a list of `Views`:

```
class CollectionView extends Backbone.View {
  render() {
    // Render a view for each model in the collection
    var html = this.collection.map(model => {
      var view = new this.modelView(model);
      view.render();
      return view.$el;
    });

    // Put the rendered items in the DOM
    this.$el.html(html);
```

```
      return this;
   }
}
```

Note that the `modelView` property should be a View class; it could be our `ModelView` class of the previous section or any other view. See how for each model in the collection it instantiates and renders a `this.modelView` with the current model. As a result, an `html` variable will contain an array of all rendered views. Finally the `html` array can be attached easily to the `$el` element.

For an example of how to use `CollectionView`, see the following example:

```
class MyModelView extends ModelView {
  // ...
)

class MyView extends CollectionView {
  constructor(options) {
    super(options);
    this.el = '#main';
    this.modelView = MyModelView;
  }
}

var view = new MyView({collection: someCollection});
view.render();
```

This snippet will do the job, it will render a `MyModelView` for each model in the `someCollection` object and put the result list in the `#main` element.

However, if you add models to the collection or remove them, the view will not be updated. That's not a desirable behavior. When a model is added, it should add a new view at the end of the list; if a model is deleted from the collection, the view associated with that model should be deleted.

A quick and dirty way to sync collection changes and views is to re-render the entire view on every change in the collection, but this approach is very inefficient because client resources are consumed when re-rendering views that don't need to change. A better approach should exist.

Adding new models

When a model is added to the collection an add event is triggered; we can create an event handler to update the view:

```
class CollectionView extends Backbone.View {
  initialize() {
    this.listenTo(this.collection, 'add', this.addModel);
  }

  // ...
}
```

When the addModel method is called, it should create and render a new view with the data of the model added and put it at the end of the list.

```
var CollectionView = Backbone.View.extend({
  // ...
  // Render a model when is added to the collection
  modelAdded(model) {
    var view = this.renderModel(model);
    this.$el.append(view.$el);
  }

  render() {
    // Render a view for each model in the collection
    var html = this.collection.map(model => {
      var view = this.renderModel(model);
      return view.$el;
    });

    // Put the rendered items in the DOM
    this.$el.html(html);
    return this;
  }

  renderModel(model) {
    // Create a new view instance, modelView should be
    // redefined as a subclass of Backbone.View
    var view = new this.modelView({model: model});

    // Keep track of which view belongs to a model
    this.children[model.cid] = view;

    // Re-trigger all events in the children views, so that
```

```
        // you can listen events of the children views from the
        // collection view
        this.listenTo(view, 'all', eventName => {
          this.trigger('item:' + eventName, view, model);
        });

        view.render();
        return view;
    }
  }
```

A `renderModel()` method was added since both methods, `render()` and `modelAdded()`, need to render the model in the same way. The DRY principle was applied.

When a child view is rendered, it is useful to listen for all the events for the given view, so that we can listen for child events from the collection.

```
var myCollectionView = new CollectionView({...});

myCollectionView.on('item:does:something', (view, model) => {
  // Do something with the model or the view
});
```

Our event handler is very simple; it renders the added model with the `renderModel()` method, attaches an event handler for any event in the view, and appends the result at the end of the DOM element.

Deleting models

When a model is removed from the collection, the view that contains that model should be deleted from the DOM to reflect the current state of the collection. Consider an event handler for the `removed` event:

```
function modelRemoved(model) {
    var view = getViewForModel(model); // Find view for this model
    view.destroy();
}
```

How can we obtain the view associated with the model? There is no easy way to do it with the code that we have. To make it easy, we can keep track of model-view associations; in this way, getting the view is very easy:

```
class CollectionView extends Backbone.View {
    initialize() {
```

```
        this.children = {};
        this.listenTo(this.collection, 'add', this.modelAdded);
        this.listenTo(this.collection, 'remove', this.modelRemoved);
    }

    // ...

    // Close view of model when is removed from the collection
    modelRemoved(model) {
        var view = this.children[model.cid];

        if (view) {
            view.remove();
            this.children[model.cid] = undefined;
        }
    }

    // ...

    renderModel(model) {
        // Create a new view instance, modelView should be
        // redefined as a subclass of Backbone.View
        var view = new this.modelView({model: model});

        // Keep track of which view belongs to a model
        this.children[model.cid] = view;

        // Re-trigger all events in the children views, so that
        // you can listen events of the children views from the
        // collection view
        this.listenTo(view, 'all', eventName => {
            this.trigger('item:' + eventName, view, model);
        });

        view.render();
        return view;
    }
}
```

At rendering time, we store a reference to the view in the `this.children` hash table for future reference, since `render()` and `modelAdded()` use the same method to render; this change is done in one place, the `renderModel()` method.

When a model is removed, the `modelRemoved()` method can easily find the view and remove it by calling the standard `remove()` method and destroying the reference in the `this.children` hash.

Destroying views

When a `CollectionView` is destroyed, it should remove all children views to clean the memory properly. This should be done by extending the `remove()` method:

```
class CollectionView extends Backbone.View {
  // ...

  // Close view of model when is removed from the collection
  modelRemoved(model) {
    if (!model) return;

    var view = this.children[model.cid];
    this.closeChildView(view);
  }

  // ...

  // Called to close the collection view, should close
  // itself and all the live childrens
  remove() {
    Backbone.View.prototype.remove.call(this);
    this.closeChildren();
  }

  // Close all the live childrens
  closeChildren() {
    var children = this.children || {};

    // Use the arrow function to bind correctly the "this" object
    _.each(children, child => this.closeChildView(child));
  }

  closeChildView(view) {
    // Ignore if view is not valid
    if (!view) return;

    // Call the remove function only if available
    if (_.isFunction(view.remove)) {
      view.remove();
```

```
    }

    // Remove event handlers for the view
    this.stopListening(view);

    // Stop tracking the model-view relationship for the
    // closed view
    if (view.model) {
      this.children[view.model.cid] = undefined;
    }
  }
}
}
```

Now, when the view needs to be removed, it will do it and clean all the children views.

Resetting the collection

When a collection is wiped, the view should re-render the entire collection, because all items were replaced:

```
class CollectionView extends Backbone.View {
  initialize() {
    // ...
    this.listenTo(this.collection, 'reset', this.render);
  }

  // ...
}
```

This works, but previous views should be closed too; as we saw in the previous section, the best place to do it is in the render method:

```
class CollectionView extends Backbone.View.extend({
  // ...
  render () {
    // Clean up any previous elements rendered
    this.closeChildren();

    // Render a view for each model in the collection
    var html = this.collection.map(model => {
      var view = this.renderModel(model);
      return view.$el;
    });

    // Put the rendered items in the DOM
```

```
        this.$el.html(html);
        return this;
    }

    // ...
}
```

If a view has no items yet, the `closeChildren()` method will not do anything.

Region

A common use case is to swap between views in a common DOM element; this can be done by using the same `el` property in both views and calling the `render()` method on the view you want to see. But this way doesn't clean the memory and event bindings because both views will remain live in memory, even if they are not in the DOM.

A particularly useful scenario is when you need to switch between sub-applications, because sub-applications are rendered in the same DOM element normally. For example, when a user wants to edit contact information, he/she will click on an **Edit** button, and the current view will be replaced with an edit form.

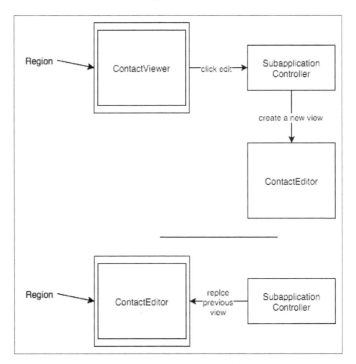

Figure 2.2: Swapping views with regions

To switch between views, a `Region` class could be used as shown next:

```
var mainRegion = new Region({el: '#main'});
var contactViewer = new ContactViewer({model: contact});

contactViewer.on('edit:contact', function(contact) {
  var editContact = new EditContactView({ model: contact });
  mainRegion.show(editContact);
});


mainRegion.show(contactViewer);
```

The `Region` object points to an existing DOM element; to show a view on that element, the `show()` method should be called on the `Region` object. Note that views don't have the `el` property set because regions will put the element in the DOM and not the View itself. This gives us an extra feature, views don't need to set an `el` property anymore and can be rendered on any available region.

A basic region manager can be implemented with this code:

```
class Region {
  constructor(options) {
    this.el = options.el;
  }

  // Closes any active view and render a new one
  show(view) {
    this.closeView(this.currentView);
    this.currentView = view;
    this.openView(view);
  }

  closeView(view) {
    // Only remove the view when the remove function
    // is available
    if (view && view.remove) {
      view.remove();
    }
  }

  openView(view) {
    // Be sure that this.$el exists
    this.ensureEl();

    // Render the view on the this.$el element
```

```
      view.render();
      this.$el.html(view.el);
    }

    // Create the this.$el attribute if do not exists
    ensureEl() {
      if (this.$el) return;
      this.$el = $(this.el);
    }

    // Close the Region and any view on it
    remove() {
      this.closeView(this.currentView);
    }
  }
```

When the `show()` method is called, it closes the current view, if any, then assigns a new `currentView` and opens the view. When a view is open, `Region` ensures that the `$el` property exists, first calling the `ensureEl()` method. Then the interesting part happens:

```
view.render();
this.$el.html(view.el);
```

The Backbone documentation explains how views works:

> *All views have a DOM element at all times (the el property), whether they've already been inserted into the page or not. In this fashion, views can be rendered at any time, and inserted into the DOM all at once [...]*

And that's what happens here: we render the view in memory first, calling `view. render()`, and then insert the result in the DOM pointed by the Region `$el` property.

A `remove()` method is implemented too, to make regions compatible with Backbone Views. When a region is removed, it needs to close the owned view too, so this allows us to do this easily.

Imagine that we have a region that owns a `CollectionView` with many views inside; when the `remove()` method is called on the region, it will call the `remove()` method on the `CollectionView`, which will call the `remove()` method on every child view.

Layout

A Layout is used to define structure; its intention is to create a skeleton where other views will be placed. A common web application layout is composed of a header, a sidebar, footer, and a common area, for example. With layouts we can define regions, in a declarative way, where these elements will be placed. After the layout is rendered, we can show the views we want on those views.

In the following figure, we can see a layout; each of these elements is a region, so other views should be created to fill the regions — for example, a HeaderView class for the header region:

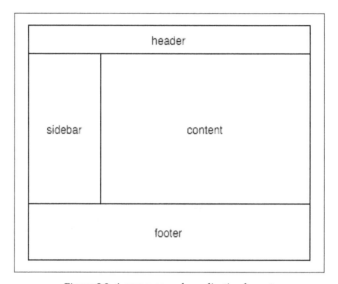

Figure 2.3: A common web application layout

An implementation of this example could be something like this:

```
var AppLayout = new Layout({
  template: $('#app-layout').html(),
  regions: {
    header: 'header',
    sicebar: '#sidebar',
    footer: 'footer',
    main: '#main'
  }
});

Var layout = new AppLayout({ el: 'body' });
```

```
var header = new HeaderView();

layout.render();
layout.getRegion('header').show(header);
```

See how regions are declared: a pair of names and a selector. The layout will expose the regions through the `getRegion()` method, which receives the name of the region and returns an instance of the `Region` class that can be used as seen in the previous section.

Also note that the layout needs to define a `template` property; it should follow the same rules used in the `ModelView` implementation. That template will define the HTML where regions will be pointed.

The following code shows how to create a Layout view:

```
class Layout extends ModelView {
  render() {
    // Clean up any rendered DOM
    this.closeRegions();

    // Render the layout template
    var result = ModelView.prototype.render.call(this);

    // Creand and expose the configurated regions
    this.configureRegions();
    return result;
  }

  configureRegions() {
    var regionDefinitions = this.regions || {};

    if (!this._regions) {
      this._regions = {};
    }

    // Create the configured regions and save a reference
    // in the this._regions attribute
    _.each(regionDefinitions, (selector, name) => {
      let $el = this.$(selector);
      this._regions[name] = new Region({el: $el});
    });
  }

  // Get a Region instance for a named region
```

```
getRegion(regionName) {
  // Ensure that regions is a valid object
  var regions = this._regions || {};
  return regions[regionName];
}

// Close the layout and all the regions on it
remove(options) {
  ModelView.prototype.remove.call(this, options);
  this.closeRegions();
}

closeRegions() {
  var regions = this._regions || {};

  // Close each active region
  _.each(regions, region => {
    if (region && region.remove) region.remove();
  });
}
}
```

The layout extends directly from `ModelView` so the `render()` method acts like in `ModelView`, but extends its behavior creating the necessary regions after rendering. The `configurateRegions()` method creates a region for every region declared on the `regions` property. Associations between region names and `Region` instances are stored in the `_regions` property, to be used on future references.

When a layout is removed, it should close any region opened, so that all resources are released cleanly. That's the job of the `closeRegions()` method; it iterates over all regions created with `configurateRegions()` and calls the `remove()` method for every region.

As the regions are stored in a private property called `_regions`, a method for accessing the regions is required; the `getRegion()` method returns the region instance associated with the name of the region.

Putting it all together

We have created four simple but powerful new views types that can be used easily on projects, minimizing the effort and making less redundant code. In the next section, we will convert our contacts project into a more complex project, using what we have learned here:

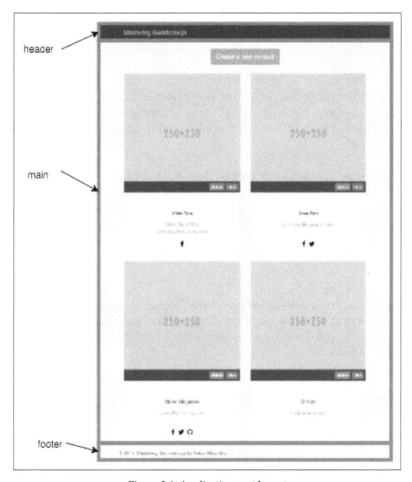

Figure 2.4: Application root layout

Our application will have a root layout with three sections:

- Header – Will contain a navigation bar
- Footer – Copyright information
- Main – This element shows all sub-applications on demand

This layout description is not a Layout object; instead, it describes the HTM root content:

```html
<!doctype html>
<html lang="">
  <head>
    <meta charset="utf-8">
    <title>mastering backbone design</title>
    <meta name="description" content="">
    <meta name="viewport" content="width=device-width, initial-
scale=1">

    <link rel="shortcut icon" href="/favicon.ico">
    <link rel="apple-touch-icon" href="/apple-touch-icon.png">
    <!-- Place favicon.ico and apple-touch-icon.png in the root
directory -->

    <link rel="stylesheet" href="css/bootstrap.min.css">
    <link rel="stylesheet" href="css/sweetalert.css">
    <link rel="stylesheet" href="css/pnotify.custom.min.css">
    <link rel="stylesheet" href="css/font-awesome.min.css">
    <link rel="stylesheet" href="css/main.css">
  </head>
  <body>
    <!--[if lt IE 10]>
      <p class="browsehappy">You are using an <strong>outdated</
strong> browser. Please <a href="http://browsehappy.com/">upgrade your
browser</a> to improve your experience.</p>
    <![endif]-->

    <nav class="navbar">
      <div class="container">
        <div class="navbar-header">
          <a class="navbar-brand" href="#">
            Mastering Backbone.js
          </a>
        </div>
      </div>
    </nav>

    <div id="main" class="container"></div>

    <script src="js/vendor/jquery-2.1.4.min.js"></script>
    <script src="js/vendor/bootstrap.min.js"></script>
```

```
<script src="js/vendor/sweetalert.min.js"></script>
<script src="js/vendor/pnotify.custom.min.js"></script>
<script src="js/vendor/underscore-min.js"></script>
<script src="js/vendor/backbone-min.js"></script>

    </body>
</html>
```

In this root layout, the header and footer are very straightforward, so is not necessary to create a separate view for them. There is a `main` div that will be our main region, for the whole application.

Showing a list

The `ContactList` subapplication is responsible for rendering the collection in the DOM. Thus, the `ContactList` object will instantiate the necessary views:

```
// apps/contacts/contactList.js
showList(contacts) {
  // Create the views
  var layout = new ContactListLayout();
  var actionBar = new ContactListActionBar();
  var contactList = new ContactListView({collection: contacts});

  // Show the views
  this.region.show(layout);
  layout.getRegion('actions').show(actionBar);
  layout.getRegion('list').show(contactList);

  this.listenTo(contactList, 'item:contact:delete',
    this.deleteContact);
}
```

A layout is created to put the `CollectionView` inside; the layout template has a `div` with a `contact-list-layout` id that will be used as the target region:

```
// index.html
<script id="contact-list-layout" type="text/template">
  <div class="actions-bar-container"></div>
  <div class="list-container"></div>
  <div class="footer text-muted">
    © 2015. <a href="#">Mastering Backbone.js</a> by <a href="https://
twitter.com/abieealejandro" target="_blank">Abiee Alejandro</a>
  </div>
</script>
```

And the layout code is very simple:

```
// apps/contacts/contactList.js
class ContactListLayout extends Layout {
  constructor(options) {
    super(options);
    this.template = '#contact-list-layout';
    this.regions = {
      actions: '.actions-bar-container',
      list: '.list-container'
    };
  }

  get className() {
    return 'row page-container';
  }
}
```

The view that renders the collection of contacts is very straightforward because it just need to specify the `modelView` attribute:

```
// apps/contacts/contactList.js
class ContactListView extends CollectionView {
  constructor(options) {
    super(options);
    this.modelView = ContactListItemView;
  }

  get className() {
    return 'contact-list';
  }
}
```

The contact card template shows the contact name, phone number, email, and its social networks:

```
// index.html
<script id="contact-list-item" type="text/template">
  <div class="box thumbnail">
    <div class="photo">
      <img src="http://placehold.it/250x250"
        alt="Contact photo" />
      <div class="action-bar clearfix">
        <div class="action-buttons pull-right">
          <button id="delete"
```

```
        class="btn btn-danger btn-xs">delete</button>
      <button id="view"
        class="btn btn-primary btn-xs">view</button>
    </div>
  </div>
</div>
<div class="caption-container">
  <div class="caption">
    <h5><%= name %></h5>
    <% if (phone) { %>
      <p class="phone no-margin"><%= phone %></p>
    <% } %>
    <% if (email) { %>
      <p class="email no-margin"><%= email %></p>
    <% } %>
    <div class="bottom">
      <ul class="social-networks">
        <% if (facebook) { %>
        <li>
          <a href="<%= facebook %>" title="Google Drive">
            <i class="fa fa-facebook"></i>
          </a>
        </li>
        <% } %>
        <% if (twitter) { %>
        <li>
          <a href="<%= twitter %>" title="Twitter">
            <i class="fa fa-twitter"></i>
          </a>
        </li>
        <% } %>
        <% if (google) { %>
        <li>
          <a href="<%= google %>" title="Google Drive">
            <i class="fa fa-google-plus"></i>
          </a>
        </li>
        <% } %>
        <% if (github) { %>
        <li>
          <a href="<%= github %>" title="Github">
            <i class="fa fa-github"></i>
          </a>
        </li>
```

```
            <% } %>
          </ul>
        </div>
      </div>
    </div>
  </div>
</script>
```

The `ContactListItemView` class should handle the delete and view events:

```
// apps/contacts/contactList.js
class ContactListItemView extends ModelView {
  constructor(options) {
    super(options);
    this.template = '#contact-list-item';
  }

  get className() {
    return 'col-xs-12 col-sm-6 col-md-3';
  }

  get events() {
    return {
      'click #delete': 'deleteContact',
      'click #view': 'viewContact'
    };
  }

  initialize(options) {
    this.listenTo(options.model, 'change', this.render);
  }

  deleteContact() {
    this.trigger('contact:delete', this.model);
  }

  viewContact() {
    var contactId = this.model.get('id');
    App.router.navigate(`contacts/view/${contactId}`, true);
  }
}
```

When the user clicks on the **Delete** button, the view triggers a `contact:delete` event and lets the controller handle the deletion process. Because the **View** button is simpler than the **Delete**, we can redirect the user to the contact list from the view; note that delegating this very simple task to the controller will add more overhead without benefit.

The action bar allow the user to add new users.

```
<script id="contact-list-action-bar" type="text/template">
  <button class="btn btn-lg btn-success">
    Create a new contact
  </button>
</script>
```

`ContactListActionBar` just renders its template and waits for a click on its button.

```
// apps/contacts/contactList.js
class ContactListActionBar extends ModelView {
  constructor(options) {
    super(options);
    this.template = '#contact-list-action-bar';
  }

  get className() {
    return 'options-bar col-xs-12';
  }

  get events() {
    return {
      'click button': 'createContact'
    };
  }

  createContact() {
    App.router.navigate('contacts/new', true);
  }
}
```

When the button is clicked, we redirect the user to the contact form to create a new user.

Showing the details

The contact details show a read-only version of a single contact; here you can see all the details of a given contact but no edition. The following screenshots shows how it looks:

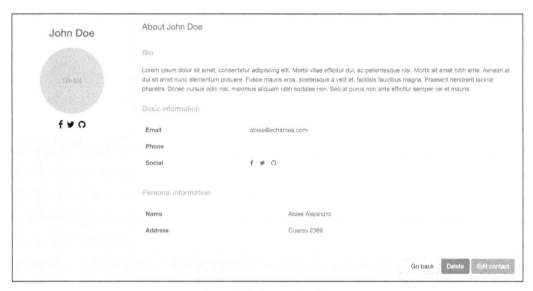

Figure 2.5: Contact details

To show a read-only version of a contact, we need to first define a layout:

```
<script id="contact-view-layout" type="text/template">
  <div class="row page-container">
    <div id="contact-widget"
      class="col-xs-12 col-sm-4 col-md-3"></div>
    <div class="col-xs-12 col-sm-8 col-md-9">
      <div class="row">
        <div id="about-container"></div>
        <div id="call-log-container"></div>
      </div>
    </div>
  </div>
  <div class="footer text-muted">
    © 2015. <a href="#">Mastering Backbone.js</a> by <a href="https://
twitter.com/abieealejandro" target="_blank">Abiee Alejandro</a>
  </div>
</script>
```

The layout defines two regions, one for the widget at the left and another one for the main content:

```
// apps/contacts/contactViewer.js
class ContactViewLayout extends Layout {
  constructor(options) {
    super(options);
    this.template = '#contact-view-layout';
    this.regions = {
      widget: '#contact-widget',
      about: '#about-container'
    };
  }

  get className() {
    return 'row page-container';
  }
}
```

When `ContactViewLayout` is rendered, the widget and the about information should be rendered. The templates for these views are very simple, so for space reasons will not be shown here; if you want to see the details of the implementation, please go to the GitHub repo for this book.

The `ContactAbout` view includes three buttons to go back to the list, another to delete the contact, and a final one to edit it.

```
// apps/contacts/contactViewer.js
class ContactAbout extends ModelView {
  constructor(options) {
    super(options);
    this.template = '#contact-view-about';
  }

  get className() {
    return 'panel panel-simple';
  }

  get events() {
    return {
      'click #back': 'goToList',
      'click #delete': 'deleteContact',
      'click #edit': 'editContact'
    };
```

```
  }

  goToList() {
    App.router.navigate('contacts', true);
  }

  deleteContact() {
    this.trigger('contact:delete', this.model);
  }

  editContact() {
    var contactId = this.model.get('id');
    App.router.navigate(`contacts/edit/${contactId}`, true);
  }
}
```

As we did in the `ContactList`, we will delegate the deletion process to the controller; views should not handle that business logic. However, the edit and go back button are simple URL redirections and can be implemented directly in the view.

Editing information

Figure 2.6 shows how the edit form for the contacts should looks. The form view should be able to grab information from the input boxes and update the Contact model passed to it.

A layout template should be created here to separate the widget at the left from the form view at the right:

```html
<script id="contact-form-layout" type="text/template">
  <div id="preview-container"
    class="col-xs-12 col-sm-4 col-md-3"></div>
  <div id="form-container"
    class="col-xs-12 col-sm-8 col-md-9"></div>

  <div class="footer text-muted">
    © 2015. <a href="#">Mastering Backbone.js</a> by <a href="http://
themeforest.net/user/Kopyov" target="_blank">Abiee Alejandro</a>
  </div>
</script>
```

Figure 2.6: Edit contact form

The layout defines two regions:

```
// apps/contacts/contactEditor.js
class ContactFormLayout extends Layout {
  constructor(options) {
    super(options);
    this.template = '#contact-form-layout';
    this.regions = {
      preview: '#preview-container',
      form: '#form-container'
    };
  }

  get className() {
    return 'row page-container';
  }
}
```

In order to edit a contact, we need to define a form:

```
// index.html
<script id="contact-form" type="text/template">
  <div class="panel panel-simple">
    <div class="panel-heading">Edit contact</div>
    <div class="panel-body">
```

```
            <form class="form-horizontal">
              <div class="form-group">
                <label for="name"
                  class="col-sm-2 control-label">Name</label>
                <div class="col-sm-10">
                  <input id="name" type="text"
                    class="form-control" placeholder="Full name"
                    value="<%= name %>" />
                </div>
              </div>
              // ...

              <hr />

              <h4>Contact info</h4>
              <div class="form-group">
                <label for="name"
                  class="col-sm-2 control-label">Phone</label>
                <div class="col-sm-10">
                  <input id="name" type="text"
                    class="form-control"
                    placeholder="(123) 456 7890" value="<%= phone %>" />
                </div>
              </div>
              // ...
            </form>
          </div>
          <div class="panel-footer clearfix">
            <div class="panel-buttons">
              <button id="cancel" class="btn btn-default">Cancel</button>
              <button id="save" class="btn btn-success">Save</button>
            </div>
          </div>
        </div>
      </script>
```

For space reasons, I have eliminated the duplicated code in the book, but you can see the complete code in the GitHub repo. Please note that this form will be used for editing and creating new contacts. For each attribute in the model, an input is rendered with the contents of the attribute:

```
// apps/contacts/contactEditor.js
class ContactForm extends ModelView {
  constructor(options) {
    super(options);
```

```
    this.template = '#contact-form';
  }

  get className() {
    return 'form-horizontal';
  }

  get events() {
    return {
      'click #save': 'saveContact',
      'click #cancel': 'cancel'
    };
  }

  serializeData() {
    return _.defaults(this.model.toJSON(), {
      name: '',
      age: '',
      phone: '',
      email: '',
      address1: '',
      address2: ''
    });
  }

  saveContact(event) {
    event.preventDefault();
    this.model.set('name', this.getInput('#name'));
    this.model.set('phone', this.getInput('#phone'));
    this.model.set('email', this.getInput('#email'));
    this.model.set('address1', this.getInput('#address1'));
    this.model.set('address2', this.getInput('#address2'));
    this.model.set('facebook', this.getInput('#facebook'));
    this.model.set('twitter', this.getInput('#twitter'));
    this.model.set('google', this.getInput('#google'));
    this.model.set('github', this.getInput('#github'));
    this.trigger('form:save', this.model);
  }

  getInput(selector) {
    return this.$el.find(selector).val();
  }

  cancel() {
```

```
        this.trigger('form:cancel');
    }
  }
```

When the user clicks on the **Cancel** button, it triggers a `form:cancel` event that is processed by the `ContactEditor` subapplication controller.

```
// apps/contacts/contactEditor.js
  cancel() {
    // Warn user before make redirection to prevent accidental
    // cencel
    App.askConfirmation('Changes will be lost', isConfirm => {
      if (isConfirm) {
        App.router.navigate('contacts', true);
      }
    });
  }
```

When the model is rendered, it may or may not contain attributes due to the server response; for this reason, we extend the `serializeData()` method to assign default values.

When the user clicks on the **Save** button, the `saveContact()` is called, it gets the data from the inputs and assigns new values to the model, then triggers a `form:save` event to be processed by the `ContactEditor` subapplication controller.

```
// apps/contacts/edit-contact.js
  saveContact(contact) {
    contact.save(null, {
      success() {
        // Redirect user to contact list after save
        App.notifySuccess('Contact saved');
        App.router.navigate('contacts', true);
      },
      error() {
        // Show error message if something goes wrong
        App.notifyError('Something goes wrong');
      }
    });
  }
```

Rendering third-party plugins

A common issue when rendering views is not rendering plugins from others because they are designed to work with traditional web applications but not with SPA; this is because many plugins are DOM-dependent, which means that the target element should exist in the actual DOM. To see this issue more clearly, let me show you an example with the jQueryUI Calendar plugin. Let's add a `birthdate` field to our `ContactEditor`, replacing the age field.

```
// index.html
// ...
<div class="form-group">
  <label for="birthdate">Birth date</label>
  <input id="birthdate " type="text"
    class="form-control" value="<%= birthdate %>" />
//...
```

And make the proper changes in the view:

```
class ContactForm extends ModelView {
  // ...
  serializeData() {
    return _.defaults(this.model.toJSON(), {
      name: '',
      birthdate: '',
      // ...
    });
  },
  saveContact(event) {
    event.preventDefault();
    this.model.set('name', this.$el.find('#name').val());
    this.model.set('birthdate',
      this.$el.find('#birthdate').val()
    );
    // ...
  },
  // ...
});
```

To show a calendar on the `birthdate` field we need to call `$('#birthdate').` `datepicker()` somewhere, but what is the best place to do that?

```
// ... edit-contact.js
class ContactEditor {
  // ...

  showEditor(contact) {
    var contactForm = new ContactForm({model: contact});
    this.region.show(contactForm);
    contactForm.$('#birthdate').datepicker();

    this.listenTo(contactForm, 'form:save', this.saveContact);
    this.listenTo(contactForm, 'form:cancel', this.cancel);
  };
};
```

After calling the `show()` method on the `region` object, the `contactForm` view is live in the DOM, so it makes sense to call the `datepicker()` method after that. However this is not a good strategy because our controller object knows about DOM elements, which are not its responsibility.

Views should be responsible for dealing with the DOM, so rendering third-party plugins is included. Another approach could be to extend the `render()` method on the `FormView` class but we already have the `onRender()` callback, which is called after the rendering process.

```
// ... edit-contact.js
var ContactForm extends ModelView {
  // ...
  onRender() {
    this.$('#birthdate').datepicker();
  },
  //...
});
```

But this is not going to work because we are rendering the view on a region. Did you remember the `show()` method?

```
class Region {
// ...
  openView(view) {
    this.ensureEl();
    view.render();
```

```
      this.$el.html(view.el);
  }
// ...
}
```

The showing process first renders the view in memory and after that makes it available on the DOM. That's why this doesn't work. The intent of the onRender() method is to make template changes before making them available on the DOM. We need to add a new callback method that will be called when the view is in the DOM.

```
class Region {
// ...
  openView(view) {
    this.ensureEl();
    view.render();
    this.$el.html(view.el);

    // Callback when the view is in the DOM
    if (view.onShow) {
      view.onShow();
    }
  }
// ...
}
```

Remember to make this feature available in CollectionView too.

```
// common.js
class CollectionView extends Backbone.View {
  // ...
  onShow() {
    var children = this.children || {};
    _.each(children, child => {
      if (child.onShow) {
        child.onShow();
      }
    });
  }
}
```

So, our `ContactForm` will end with something like this.

```
// apps/contacts/contactEditor.js
class ContactForm extends ModelView {
  // ...

  // Call the onShow method for each children
  onShow() {
    // Ensure that children exists
    var children = this.children || {};

    _.each(children, child => {
      if (child.onShow) {
        child.onShow();
      }
    });
  }
  //...
}
```

Remember, most third-party plugins need to have the element in the DOM or they will not work, so you should call the plugin only after rendering the view. The best place to call plugins is in the extended view class so the responsibility for DOM manipulation is encapsulated in the view.

Conclusions

We started by creating common view types that are common for almost every project. Those views are simple in principle but powerful; we can effectively manage nested views without worrying about insufficient memory.

We learned that, by encapsulating common patterns in the `render()` method, we can create useful view types; in this chapter, we have seen four of them but if you are curious I encourage you to take a look at the Marionette framework, which works on top of Backbone.

Marionette includes all the views exposed here: `ItemView`, `CollectionView`, `LayoutView`, Regions. and other useful view types. Marionette objects behave very similarly to what we see here, so that you can easily interchange Marionette objects with those described in this chapter.

Plugins should be called only after the view is on the DOM, because most plugins are DOM-dependent. When rendering plugins, remember to do it in the view not outside it; the `onShow()` callback strategy ensures that the view is available on the DOM, and so is the best place to render third-party plugins.

In the next chapter, you will learn more about how to sync views and models. You will see how to manage complex data and render it effectively in views. Validation is an important feature for your application; you will learn how to validate models and use that information to display error messages on your views.

3
Model Bindings

Keeping models in sync with other objects such as views can be challenging, and if it is not done correctly, it can lead to messy code. In this chapter, we will explore how to deal with data synchronization to make data binding easier. But, what is data binding? Wikipedia defines data binding as:

> *Data binding is the process that establishes a connection between the application UI (User Interface) and business logic. If the settings and notifications are correctly set, the data reflects changes when made. It can also mean that when the UI is changed, the underlying data will reflect that change.*

A common issue with model binding is how to deal with complex model structures that include other embedded objects or lists; in this chapter, we will define a strategy to deal with these scenarios. A missing feature in Backbone is two-way binding; in the next sections, we will see how to implement this without a headache.

Let's start the chapter describing how to bind model data with views manually to see how Backbone works; after that, we can use Backbone.Stickit to make it much easier. After learning how to sync model data and views, we will explore how to perform validations on the models and how to display error messages.

Manual binding

To make it simple, imagine that we have a form with a simple layout: name, phone, and an email address:

```
<script id="form-template" type="text/template">
<form>
<div class="form-group">
<label for="name">Name</label>
<input id="name" class="form-control" type="text"
value="<%= name %>" />
```

```
</div>
<div class="form-group">
<label for="phone">Name</label>
<input id="phone" class="form-control" type="text"
value="<%= phone %>" />
</div>
<div class="form-group">
<label for="email">Name</label>
<input id="email" class="form-control" type="text"
value="<%= email %>" />
</div>
<button type="submit"class="btn btn-default">Save now</button>
</form>
</script>

<script id="preview-template" type="text/template">
<h3><%= name %></h3>
<ul>
<li><%= phone %></li>
<li><%= email %></li>
</ul>
</script>
```

In the snippet, we have two views that will be rendered at the same time. When the user clicks on the **Save** button in the form, the preview template will be updated with the model data:

```
'use strict';

var contact = new Backbone.Model({
  name: 'John Doe',
  phone: '555555555',
  email: 'john.doe@example.com'
});

class FormView extends ModelView {
  constructor(options) {
    super(options);
    this.template = '#form-template';
    this.model = contact;
  }
}

class ContactPreview extends ModelView {
  constructor(options) {
```

```
      super(options);
      this.template = '#preview-template';
      this.model = contact;

      // Re-render the view if something in the model
      // changes
      this.model.on('change', this.render, this);
    }
  }

var form = new FormView({
  el: '#contact-form'
});

var preview = new ContactPreview({
  el: '#contact-preview'
});

form.render();
preview.render();
```

This code will render the contents of the `contact` model in the form and in the preview. When the **Save now** button is clicked, nothing happens because it hasn't yet been programmed, so let's save the changes in the model:

```
var FormView = ModelView.extend({
  // ...
  events() {
    return {
      'click button[type="submit"]': 'saveContact'
    };
  }

  saveContact(event) {
    event.preventDefault();
    this.model.set('name', this.$('#name').val());
    this.model.set('phone', this.$('#phone').val());
    this.model.set('email', this.$('#email').val());
  }
});
```

Let's see what's happening here. In `FormView`, we're updating the model with the data in the form inputs; this action syncs the form data with the model, triggering a `'change'` event on the Model. Because `ContactPreview` is listening for the change, the event will update itself with the data in the model.

Backbone is not built with *automagic* view-model bindings, so it's the developer's responsibility to implement it. Fortunately, there are some Backbone plugins that can help us to make it less painful; one of these is `Backbone.Stickit`, developed by the *New York Times*.

Two-way binding

`Angular.js` has been popularized as two-way data binding in the frontend; the idea behind two-way data binding is to keep views and models in sync. When you make a change in an input field the view the model should be updated immediately, and if you change a property in the model the view should show the current value immediately:

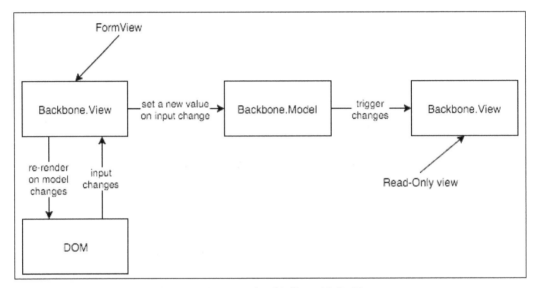

Figure 3.1 Two-way data binding with Backbone

Backbone does not provide a mechanism to achieve this easily; however, we can do it using the event system that Backbone models provide. Figure 3.1 shows how you can make an implementation.

`Backbone.View` listens for `keyup` and `change` events on input controls at the DOM; when a change is triggered from the DOM, `Backbone.View` can extract the new value from the input and set the Model:

```
class FormView extends ModelView {
    // ...

    events() {
```

```
    return {
      'click button[type="submit"]': 'saveContact',
      'keyup input': 'inputChanged',
      'change input': 'inputChanged'
    };
  }

  inputChanged(event) {
    var $target = $(event.target);
    var value = $target.val();
    var id = $target.attr('id');
    this.model.set(id, value);
  }

// ...
}
```

When you call the `set()` method on `Backbone.View`, at least two events are triggered: `change` and `change:<fieldname>`.We can use these events to update the necessary views:

```
var myModel = new Backbone.Model();

myModel.on('change:foo', event => {
  console.log('foo changed to', event.changed.foo);
});
myModel.on('change', event => {
  var changedKeys = _.keys(event.changed);

  changedKeys.forEach(key => {
    console.log(key, 'changed to', event.changed[key]);
  });
});

myModel.set('foo', 'bar');
myModel.set('baz', 'xyz');
myModel.set({
  foo: 'stuff',
  baz: 'zxy'
});
```

You can see the output of the preceding snippet in the following figure:

```
foo changed to bar
foo changed to bar
baz changed to xyz
foo changed to stuff
foo changed to stuff
baz changed to zxy
```

Figure 3.2 Output of change events

We can use these events to update the view when necessary. Indeed, the code we already have is enough to keep the ContactForm and ContactPreview views in sync.

```
this.model.on('change', this.render, this);
```

ContactPreview is listening for every change in the model and re-rendering the view when something changes. However, re-rendering the whole view each time is a heavy process; it would be better if we made the changes only when necessary.

First, you will need to identify each field with an identifier:

```
<script id="preview-template" type="text/template">
<h3 id="name"><%= name %></h3>
<ul>
<li id="phone"><%= phone %></li>
<li id="email"><%= email %></li>
</ul>
</script>
```

And the change event handler will update only the contents of the identified elements:

```
class ContactPreview extends ModelView {
  constructor(options) {
    //...

    // Re-render the view if something in the model
    // changes
    this.model.on('change', this.handleChange, this);
  }

  handleChange(event) {
    var changedKeys = _.keys(event.changed);

    changedKeys.forEach(key => {
```

```
        let $target = this.$('#' + key);
        if ($target) {
          $target.html(event.changed[key]);
        }
      });
    }
  }
```

Despite the result of the two-way data binding it should be used with caution; some people don't think that two-way data binding is a good idea and consider it as an anti-pattern.

References

Refer to the following URLs for more information:

- Why you should not use AngularJS: `http://bit.ly/1Mue1kC`
- AngularJS Antipatterns and Pitfalls: `http://bit.ly/1kTHKqS`
- What's wrong with Angular 1: `http://bit.ly/1N9wHok`

Data binding with plugins

As you can see in the previous section, Backbone does not provide an easy mechanism to sync your models and the views that use them. Some plugins for Backbone have been developed to minimize this issue; one of them is `Backbone.Stickit`.

If you want an easy and yet powerful way to bind DOM nodes and Backbone models, `Backbone.Stickit` will do a great job:

```
var FormView = ModelView.extend({
template: '#form-template',
  bindings: {
    '#name': 'name',
    '#phone': 'phone',
    '#email': 'email'
  },
  onRender: function() {
    this.stickit();
  }
});
```

The preceding code example shows how it looks; please consult the project documentation to learn more about it.

Binding embedded data

One of the most common issues with Backbone is how to deal with complex model data:

```
{
"name": "John Doe",
"address": {
"street": "Seleme",
"number": "1975 int 6",
"city": "Culiacán"
  },
"phones": [{
"label": "Home",
"number": "55 555 123"
  }, {
"label": "Office",
"number": "55 555 234"
  }],
"emails": [{
"label": "Work",
"email": "john.doe@example.com"
  }]
}
```

It could be easy to render a read-only view for this model data; however, the real challenge is how to bind form actions with embedded arrays. In Backbone, it is difficult to use the event system on array objects; if you push a new item in the list, no event will be triggered. This makes it difficult to keep model data in sync with the a view that edits its contents.

Binding an embedded list

Imagine that our Contacts App will now allow us to add more than one phone and email. We will need to change the edit form view to add support for adding, removing, and modifying items on the array of phones and emails:

Figure 3.3. Contact form layout with phone and email lists

Figure 3.3 shows the result of adding a **New** button to allow the user to dynamically add the number of phones and emails he/she wants. Each item in the list should include a **Delete** button too to allow the user to remove them.

To render the phone and email lists and sync the forms with the model, we will follow a different strategy; Figure 3.4 illustrates how our strategy will look:

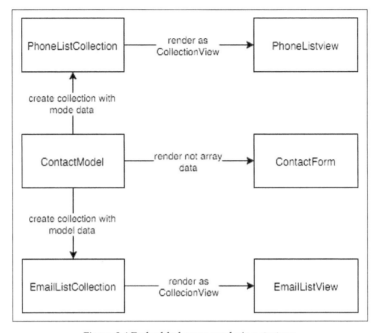

Figure 3.4 Embedded array rendering strategy

We will create two new Backbone collections, one for phones and another for emails. With the data in the Contact model we can initialize these collections and render them as regular CollectionView.

As we saw in the previous chapter, CollectionView objects take care of the changes in the collection that it renders, so that we can modify the collection object and the view will behave as expected.

When the user clicks on the **Save** button, we can serialize the content of these collections and update the model before we call the save() method.

Each item for phones and emails will have a very similar template:

```
<script id="contact-form-phone-item" type="text/template">
<div class="col-sm-4 col-md-2">
<input type="text" class="form-control description"
placeholder="home, office, mobile"
 value="<%= description %>" />
</div>
<div class="col-sm-6 col-md-8">
<input type="text" class="form-control phone"
```

```
placeholder="(123) 456 7890" value="<%= phone %>" />
</div>
<div class="col-sm-2 col-md-2 action-links">
<a href="#" class="pull-rigth delete">delete</a>
</div>
</script>
```

This template will be used as a `ModelView` for a `CollectionView`:

```js
// apps/contacts/contactEditor.js
class PhoneListItemView extends ModelView {
  constructor(options) {
    super(options);
    this.template = '#contact-form-phone-item';
  }

  get className() {
    return 'form-group';
  }
}

class PhoneListView extends CollectionView {
  constructor(options) {
    super(options);
    this.modelView = PhoneListItemView;
  }
}
```

The contact form now should include two regions for `PhoneListView` and `EmailListView`:

```html
<div class="panel panel-simple">
<div class="panel-heading">
    Phones
<button id="new-phone"
class="btn btn-primary btn-sm pull-right">New</button>
</div>
<div class="panel-body">
<form class="form-horizontal phone-list-container"></form>
</div>
</div>

<div class="panel panel-simple">
<div class="panel-heading">
    Emails
```

```
<button id="new-email"
 class="btn btn-primary btn-sm pull-right">New</button>
</div>
<div class="panel-body">
<form class="form-horizontal email-list-container"></form>
</div>
</div>
```

ContactForm should be changed to support regions; we will extend from Layout instead of ModelView:

```
// apps/contacts/contactEditor.js
class ContactForm extends Layout {
  constructor(options) {
    super(options);
    this.template = '#contact-form';
    this.regions = {
      phones: '.phone-list-container',
      emails: '.email-list-container'
    };
  }

  // ...
}
```

We will need two new models: Phone and Email. Because both models are very similar, I will only show Phone:

```
// apps/contacts/models/phone.js
'use strict';

App.Models = App.Models || {};

class Phone extends Backbone.Model {
  get defaults() {
    return {
      description: '',
      phone: ''
    };
  }
}

App.Models.Phone = Phone;
```

And collection that uses the `Phone` model:

```
// apps/contacts/collections/phoneCollection.js
'use strict';

App.Collections = App.Collections || {};

class PhoneCollection extends Backbone.Collection {
  constructor(options) {
    super(options);
  }

  get model() {
    return App.Models.Phone;
  }
}

App.Collections.PhoneCollection = PhoneCollection;
```

Now that we have the necessary objects to render the form, let's put them all together in the controller. First, we need to create the collection instances from the model data:

```
// apps/contacts/contactEditor.js
class ContactEditor {
  // ...

  showEditor(contact) {
// Data
    var phonesData = contact.get('phones') || [];
    var emailsData = contact.get('emails') || [];
this.phones = new App.Collections.PhoneCollection(phonesData);
this.emails = new App.Collections.EmailCollection(emailsData);

    // ...
  }

  // ...
}
```

With the collections in place, we can build `CollectionViews` properly:

```
// apps/contacts/contactEditor.js
class ContactEditor {
  // ...

  showEditor(contact) {
    // ...

    // Create the views
    var layout = new ContactFormLayout({model: contact});
    var phonesView = new PhoneListView({collection: this.phones});
    var emailsView = new EmailListView({collection: this.emails});
    var contactForm = new ContactForm({model: contact});
    var contactPreview = new ContactPreview({model: contact});

    // ...
  }

  // ...
}
```

The `phonesView` and `emailsView` can be rendered in the regions exposed in the `contactForm` object:

```
// apps/contacts/contactEditor.js
class ContactEditor {
  // ...

  showEditor(contact) {
    // ...

    // Render the views
    this.region.show(layout);
    layout.getRegion('form').show(contactForm);
    layout.getRegion('preview').show(contactPreview);
    contactForm.getRegion('phones').show(phonesView);
    contactForm.getRegion('emails').show(emailsView);

    // ...
  }

  // ...
}
```

When the user clicks on the **New** button, a new item in a proper list should be added:

```
// apps/contacts/contactEditor.js
class ContactForm extends Layout {
  // ...

  get events() {
    return {
      'click #new-phone': 'addPhone',
      'click #new-email': 'addEmail',
      'click #save': 'saveContact',
      'click #cancel': 'cancel'
    };
  }

  addPhone() {
    this.trigger('phone:add');
  }

  addEmail() {
    this.trigger('email:add');
  }

  // ...
}
```

The ContactForm knows nothing about the collections that we are using in the controller, so they can't add an item in the collection directly; the controller should listen for events in the contactForm and update the collection:

```
// apps/contacts/contactEditor.js
class ContactEditor {
  // ...

  showEditor(contact) {
    // ...

    this.listenTo(contactForm, 'phone:add', this.addPhone);
    this.listenTo(contactForm, 'email:add', this.addEmail);


    // ...
  }

  addPhone() {
```

```
        this.phones.add({});
    }

    addEmail() {
        this.emals.add({});
    }

    // ...
}
```

When the user clicks on the **delete** link in an item of the list, the item should be removed from the collection:

```
// apps/contacts/contactEditor.js
class PhoneListItemView extends ModelView {
    //...

    get events() {
        return {
            'click a': 'deletePhone'
        };
    }

    deletePhone(event) {
        event.preventDefault();
        this.trigger('phone:deleted', this.model);
    }
}
```

As we did with add, the controller will take care of managing the collection data by attaching an event listener in the list view:

```
// apps/contacts/contactEditor.js
class ContactEditor {
    // ...

    showEditor(contact) {
        // ...

        this.listenTo(phonesView, 'item:phone:deleted',
(view, phone) => {
this.deletePhone(phone);
}
);
        this.listenTo(emailsView, 'item:email:deleted',
```

```
  (view, email) => {
this.deleteEmail(email);
}
);

    // ...
  }

  deletePhone(phone) {
    this.phones.remove(phone);
  }

  deleteEmail(email) {
    this.emails.remove(email);
  }

  // ...
}
```

As you can see in the preceding snippets, adding items to the list (and removing them) is pretty simple; we just need to update the underlying collection and the views will be updated automatically. We did a great job with `CollectionViews` in the previous chapter.

To save the phone and email attributes in the model, we need to extract the data stored in the collections and replace the existing data in the model:

```
// apps/contacts/contactEditor.js
class ContactEditor {
  // ...

  saveContact(contact) {
    var phonesData = this.phones.toJSON();
    var emailsData = this.emails.toJSON();

    contact.set({
      phones: phonesData,
      emails: emailsData
    });

    contact.save(null, {
      success() {
        // Redirect user to contact list after save
        App.notifySuccess('Contact saved');
        App.router.navigate('contacts', true);
```

```
      },
      error() {
        // Show error message if something goes wrong
        App.notifyError('Something goes wrong');
      }
    });
  }
  // ...
}
```

However, the collections are not in sync with the forms and you will end up with empty emails and phones. To fix this, we need to bind the models with the inputs:

```
// apps/contacts/contactEditor.js
class PhoneListItemView extends ModelView {
  // ...

  get events() {
    return {
      'change .description': 'updateDescription',
      'change .phone': 'updatePhone',
      'click a': 'deletePhone'
    };
  }

  updateDescription() {
    var $el = this.$('.description');
    this.model.set('description', $el.val());
  }

  updatePhone() {
    var $el = this.$('.phone');
    this.model.set('phone', $el.val());
  }

  // ...
}
```

Now, if you click the **Save** button, the data about the phones and emails will be stored as expected.

This way of binding embedded arrays in views through intermediate collections simplifies the way you work with lists and will make your code a lot simpler and more maintainable.

Validating model data

Usually, on frontend applications, the inputs are validated with UI plugins such as jQuery Validation, which focuses on the user interface. In other words, the data is validated directly on the DOM. However, on bigger applications that would not be the best approach.

Validations in Backbone can be done manually or through plugins. Of course, the best approach is to use a plugin because it saves time and effort, but before we learn how to use the `backbone.validation` plugin, I want to show you how native validation works.

Manual validation

Backbone models have three properties to help us validate the model data: `validate()`, `validationError()`, and `isValid()`. The `validate()` method should return nothing if the model data is correct, or a value otherwise.

Backbone leaves open what should be returned by the `validate()` method, so you can return just a plain string message or a complex object:

```
class Chapter extends Backbone.Model{
  validate(attrs, options) {
    if (attrs.end < attrs.start) {
      return "can't end before it starts";
    }
  }
}
```

You can call the `isValid()` method to ensure that your model has a valid state; internally, Backbone will call the `validate()` method and will return a Boolean value depending on the returned value: `true` if `validate()` returns nothing, `false` if it returns something.

With `validationError`, you can get the latest validation error in the model—for example:

```
var one = new Chapter({
  title : "Chapter One: The Beginning",
  start: 15,
  end: 10
});

If (!one.isValid()) {
  alert(one.validationError);
}
```

The `validate()` method is called by Backbone when you want to save the model, and will trigger an `'invalid'` event if the model is not valid:

```
one.on("invalid", function(model, error) {
  alert(model.get("title") + " " + error);
});

one.save({
  start: 15,
  end: 10
});
```

In the contacts editor, we are not validating anything. It's time to start with some validations; let's validate the name of the contact:

```
// apps/contacts/models/contact.js
var Contact extends Backbone.Model {
  validate(attrs) {
    if(_.isEmpty(attrs.name)) {
      return {
        attr: 'name',
        message: 'name is required'
      };
    }
  }
}

var contact = new Contact({
// ...
});
```

Remember, the `validate()` method can return anything. Backbone will assume that the model is valid only if `validate()` does not return something. In this case, an object is returned. Objects are more useful that plain string, because return more information that can be used for a better user experience.

When an error occurs an `'invalid'` event will be triggered. The editor form should display the error, so that the form will be listening for the `'invalid'` event in the model, and managing the DOM to display error messages:

```
// apps/contacts/contactEditor.js
class ContactForm extends Layout {
  constructor(options) {
    super(options);
    this.template = '#contact-form';
    this.regions = {
```

```
      phones: '.phone-list-container',
      emails: '.email-list-container'
    };

    this.listenTo(this.model, 'invalid', this.showError);
  }

// ...

  showError(model, error) {
    this.clearErrors();

    var selector = '#' + error.attr;
    var $msg = $('<span>')
      .addClass('error')
      .addClass('help-block')
      .html(error.message);
    this.$(selector)
      .closest('.form-group')
      .addClass('has-error');
    this.$(selector)
      .after($msg);
  }

  clearErrors() {
    this.$('.has-error').removeClass('has-error');
    this.$('span.error').remove();
  }
}
```

The `showError()` method appends a `span` message below the input box, so the user can see what's wrong. With the `attr` property in the error object, we can put the error message in the right box; that's why using an error object is better than plain-text messages.

Note that we are creating a DOM element in the `showError()` method. I'm creating the element dynamically to simplify the code in the view. Of course, you can create a `span` element directly in the template too and show/hide it as needed.

Validating with the Backbone.Validation plugin

`Backbone.Validation` simplifies the validation process, allowing us to write validation rules in a declarative way instead of programmatically. Also, it comes with built-in validation rules that you can use out-of-the-box. When using `Backbone.Validation`, the way you validate models is simplified, as we will show next.

To start with `Backbone.Validation`, install the plugin after including Backbone.

```
<script src="js/vendor/backbone.js"></script>
<script src="js/vendor/backbone-validation.js"></script>
```

Now we can use the plugin; `Backbone.Validation` uses a validation property in the models to specify validation rules:

```
class Contactextends Backbone.Model {
get validation: {
    name: {
      required: true,
      minLength: 3
    }
  }
}
```

Instead of using the `validate()` method, you can write the validation rules in a configuration object, where the keys of the object are the name of the fields in the model; in this case, we are validating the `name` field. The `required` and `minLength` validation rules are applied to the `name` field by `Backbone.Validation`.

Now that the `Contact` model has the validation configuration, we need to override the default `validate()` method in the Backbone model to activate the `Backbone.Validation` plugin. To do it, we need to call the `Backbone.Validation.bind()` method in the `onRender()` method:

```
class ContactForm extends Layout {
// ...

  onRender() {
    Backbone.Validation.bind(this);
  }

  // ...
});
```

The showError() and clearErrors() are now unnecessary because we override the validate() method on the model. The Backbone.Validation plugin provides hooks to tell you when a model is valid; we will use these hooks as a shortcut. For now, the save:contact handler should change to invoke the isValid() method:

```
formLayout.on('save:contact', function() {
  if (!contact.isValid(true)) {
    return;
  }
  contact.unset('phones', { silent: true });
  contact.set('phones', phoneCollection.toJSON());
});
```

Note the true argument in the isValid() method; this argument should be used to validate all the model attributes.

When Backbone.Validation detects that a field is invalid, it will try to show an error message in the form; however, the default behavior is based on the name attribute in the form inputs. You can change the default behavior to show errors properly in our layout:

```
// app.js
_.extend(Backbone.Validation.callbacks, {
  valid(view, attr) {
    var $el = view.$('#' + attr);
    if ($el.length === 0) {
      $el = view.$('[name~=' + attr + ']');
    }

    // If input is inside an input group, $el is changed to
    // remove error properly
    if ($el.parent().hasClass('input-group')) {
      $el = $el.parent();
    }

    var $group = $el.closest('.form-group');
    $group.removeClass('has-error')
      .addClass('has-success');

    var $helpBlock = $el.next('.help-block');
    if ($helpBlock.length === 0) {
      $helpBlock = $el.children('.help-block');
    }
    $helpBlock.slideUp({
      done: function() {
```

```
            $helpBlock.remove();
        }
    });
},

invalid(view, attr, error) {
    var $el = view.$('#' + attr);
    if ($el.length === 0) {
        $el = view.$('[name~=' + attr + ']');
    }

    $el.focus();

    var $group = $el.closest('.form-group');
    $group.removeClass('has-success')
        .addClass('has-error');

    // If input is inside an input group $el is changed to
    // place error properly
    if ($el.parent().hasClass('input-group')) {
        $el = $el.parent();
    }

    // If error already exists and its message is different to new
    // error's message then the previous one is replaced,
    // otherwise new error is shown with a slide down animation
    if ($el.next('.help-block').length !== 0) {
        $el.next('.help-block')[0].innerText = error;
    } else if ($el.children('.help-block').length !== 0) {
        $el.children('.help-block')[0].innerText = error;
    } else {
        var $error = $('<div>')
                        .addClass('help-block')
                        .html(error)
                        .hide();

        // Placing error
        if ($el.prop('tagName') === 'div' &&
!$el.hasClass('input-group')) {
            $el.append($error);
        } else {
```

```
        $el.after($error);
    }

    // Showing animation on error message
    $error.slideDown();
   }
  }
});
```

The `invalid()` method will be called when invalid data is found; the callback is called with an instance of the view, the field name that has the invalid data, and a message. With that information, we can create a `span` error message and add the `has-error` class to the `control-group` that contains the input.

Please consult the `Backbone.Validation` documentation to learn more about its advantages and usage.

Summary

In this chapter, we learned how to keep models and views in sync. In general, syncing model and views is easy but things can turn difficult if the model has embedded arrays. You can use a plugin to simplify the data binding; `Backbone.Stickit` is a good option because it allows you to make your bindings in a declarative way.

I showed you how you can make two-way data binding with a vanilla Backbone, taking advantage of the event system; it's not always a good idea to use intensive two-way data binding in your applications but in some cases it can be useful.

Finally, we learned how to validate models with Backbone and how to use the validation API to show error messages in views. The `Backbone.Validation` plugin can help you to validate Backbone models easily with minimal effort, once validation callbacks are set correctly.

In the next chapter, we will learn how to modularize our contacts application to make it more maintainable and more effectively manage dependencies. Then we will bundle the whole application in a single script to load it faster.

4
Modular Code

As your project's code grows, the number of scripts in the project will be more and more, incrementing script-loading complexity. The classic way to load JavaScript files is to write a`<script>` tags for every script you have, but you have to do it in the right order; if you don't, your code could stop working. That's not an efficient way for medium-size projects.

What happens if you forget the order of loading? What if you make a refactorization on the code and the order of the script changes? It will be a pain to fix it and keep track of all the code and its dependencies.

This problem has been addressed in different ways. One is to create a module syntax to create, load, and declare explicitly the dependencies of modules; the syntax is called **AMD (Asynchronous Module Definition)**. The AMD modules define a list of module dependencies, and the code inside the module will be executed only after the dependencies are fully loaded.

The dependencies are loaded asynchronously; that means that you don't need to load all the scripts in the HTML page through `<script>` tags. AMD modules are better than plain JavaScript because they define dependencies explicitly and can be loaded automatically.

Although AMD modules are better than `<script>` tags, working with AMD modules can be a pain when unit testing comes in because you need to know the intricacies of how the library loads the modules; when you want to do unit testing, you need to isolate the pieces of code under test, but is hard to do it in RequireJS, and even if you do it the result can be buggy.

Recently another module loader and dependency manager has arrived; Browserify seems to be the most popular at the moment. However, it is not the only one; there are many other potentially strong choices such as jspm and steal.js.

In this book, we will work with Browserify because of its popularity, so you can find a lot of information and documentation about it on the Web; another good reason is that many projects have been built with it, which demonstrates its maturity and that it's production-ready. Browserify uses the same Node module syntax to define modules and dependencies, so that if you already know about Node you can go directly to the Browserify section.

CommonJS modules

In recent years, Node has been gaining popularity in the software industry; indeed it is becoming a very popular choice for backend development in a full JavaScript technology stack. If you don't know about Node, you can think about it as JavaScript used in the server instead of a browser.

Node uses the CommonJS module syntax for its modules; a CommonJS module is a file that exports a single value to be used for other modules. It is useful to use CommonJS because it provides a clean way to manage JavaScript modules and dependencies.

To support CommonJS, Node uses the `require()` function. With `require()` you can load JavaScript files without the need to use `<script>` tags, instead calling `require()` with the name of the module/dependency that you need and assigning it to a variable.

To illustrate how CommonJS modules work, let's write a Node module and see how to use the `require()` function. The following code shows a simple module that exposes a simple object with the method `sayHello()`:

```
hello = {
  sayHello(name) {
    name = name || 'world';
    console.log('hello', name);
  }
}

module.exports = hello;
```

This script can be placed in a file named `hello.js`, for example. The hello module can be loaded from another module by calling the `require()` function, as shown in the following code:

```
var hello = require('./hello');
hello.sayHello('world'); // prints "hello world"
```

When we require a script with the `require()` function we don't need to add the .js extension, Node will do it for us automatically. Note that, if you add the extension to the script name, Node will add the extension anyway and you will get an error because the `hello.js.js` file does not exist.

That's the way you can define CommonJS modules for your projects: we just export the variable that we want to expose to the outside of the module with `module.exports` and then load the module where needed with `require()`.

CommonJS modules are singletons, which means that every time you load a module you will get the same instance of the object. Node will cache the returned value when it's called for the first time and will reuse it for the next calls.

NPM and package.json

With Browserify, we can create CommonJS modules that can be executed in the browser. When you use CommonJS modules in the browser, Browserify will provide the necessary tools to load the modules, which includes a definition for the `require()` function.

When you use Browserify, you can use the Node package manager to install and define dependencies for your projects. A useful tool is the npm command tool, used to install and manage project dependencies.

The `package.json` file in a Node project is a JSON file used to define, install, and manage the version of the libraries that your project depends on. A `package.json` file can contain many configuration options; you can see the complete documentation on the Node website at `https://docs.npmjs.com/`. Here is a list of the main values.

- `Name` – The name of the project without spaces
- `Description` – A short description of the project
- `Version` – A version number for the project, typically starting with 0.0.1
- `Dependencies` – A list of libraries with the version number that the project depends on
- `devDependencies` – Same as dependencies, but this list is used only for development environments — useful for putting libraries for testing, for instance
- `licence` – A license name for the project code

We can start with a very simple `package.json` file that contains only some basic fields, and then we can extend it as needed:

```
{
  "name": "backbone-contacts ",
  "version": "0.0.1",
  "description": "Example code for the book Mastering Backbone.js",
  "author": "Abiee Alejandro <abiee.alejandro@gmail.com>",
  "license": "ISC",
  "dependencies": {
  },
  "devDependencies": {
  }
}
```

As you can see, we don't have any dependency yet. We can install our first dependency with npm:

```
$ npm install --save underscore jquery backbone bootstrap
```

This command will install the basic dependencies to work with `backbone`; the save flag will update automatically the `package.json` file, adding the library names and its current versions:

```
"dependencies": {
  "backbone": "^1.2.1",
  "bootstrap": "^3.3.5",
  "jquery": "^2.1.4",
  "underscore": "^1.8.3"
}
```

The format of the library version follows the semver standard; you can see more about this format in the official semver website.

One advantage of using the `package.json` file in your project is that, the next time you want to install the dependencies, you don't need to remember the libraries and their versions; you can just hit **Install** without any argument and Node will read the `package.json` file and make the installs for you:

```
$ npm install
```

With npm you can install development packages such as the mocha testing library, but instead of using the save flag use `save-dev`:

```
$ npm install --save-dev mocha
```

Now that you know how to install dependencies and save them in the `package.json` file, we can start using Browserify in the Contacts app.

Browserify

With Browserify we can use Node modules directly in the browser. This means that you can build your projects with the power of the npm package manager and the Node module syntax exposed in the previous sections. Then Browserify can take your source code and apply some transformations to be able to run your code in the browser environment.

A very simple module that exposes an object with a method that prints a hello message can be written as a Node module:

```
// hello.js
module.exports = {
  sayHello: function(name) {
    name = name || 'world';
    console.log('hello', name);
  }
}
```

This simple piece of code can be loaded from another script as shown next:

```
// main.js
var hello = require('./hello');
hello.sayHello();          // hello world
hello.sayHello('abiee');   // hello abiee
```

This code works perfectly with Node. You can run it as follows:

```
$ node main.js
```

However this code will not run in the browser because the `require` function and the module object are not defined. Browserify takes your project entry code and tracks all the dependencies to create a single file with all the scripts concatenated:

```
$ browserify main.js
(function e(t,n,r){function s(o,u){if(!n[o]){if(!t[o]){var a=typeof
require=="function"&&require;if(!u&&a)return a(o,!0);if(i)return
i(o,!0);var f=new Error("Cannot find module '"+o+"'");throw
f.code="MODULE_NOT_FOUND",f}var l=n[o]={exports:{}};t[o][0].
call(l.exports,function(e){var n=t[o][1][e];return s(n?n:e)},l,l.
exports,e,t,n,r)}return n[o].exports}var i=typeof require=="function"&
&require;for(var o=0;o<r.length;o++)s(r[o]);return s})({1:[function(re
quire,module,exports){
module.exports = {
  sayHello: function(name) {
    name = name || 'world';
    console.log('hello', name);
```

```
    }
  }

},{}],2:[function(require,module,exports){
var hello = require('./hello');

hello.sayHello();
hello.sayHello('abiee');

},{"./hello":1}]},{},[2]);
```

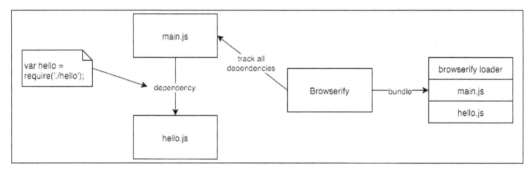

Figure 4.1 Bundling with Browserify

Note that our code is still in there; Browserify makes the definition of the missing objects and concatenates all the script in a single file. Figure 4.1 shows a graphical representation of what happens. If you use libraries such as Backbone, then your final script will contain all the Backbone code in the output file.

To tell Browserify that you want to create a file instead of just putting the result in the standard output, use the -o flag:

$ browserify main.js -o app.js

That will create an app.js file with the contents of the hello.js and main.js files.

Application dependency

When the application is loaded in the browser, it loads all the JavaScript files in a specific order. The order is important because it represents the chain of dependencies.

```
<script src="js/vendor/jquery-2.1.4.min.js"></script>
<script src="js/vendor/bootstrap.min.js"></script>
<script src="js/vendor/sweetalert.min.js"></script>
<script src="js/vendor/jquery.noty.packaged.min.js"></script>
```

```html
<script src="js/vendor/underscore-min.js"></script>
<script src="js/vendor/backbone-min.js"></script>
<script src="js/vendor/backbone-validation-min.js"></script>

<script src="js/common.js"></script>
<script src="js/app.js"></script>
<script src="js/apps/contacts/router.js"></script>
<script src="js/apps/contacts/models/contact.js"></script>
<script src="js/apps/contacts/models/phone.js"></script>
<script src="js/apps/contacts/models/email.js"></script>
<script src="js/apps/contacts/collections/contactCollection.js"></script>
<script src="js/apps/contacts/collections/phoneCollection.js"></script>
<script src="js/apps/contacts/collections/emailCollection.js"></script>
<script src="js/apps/contacts/contactList.js"></script>
<script src="js/apps/contacts/contactViewer.js"></script>
<script src="js/apps/contacts/contactEditor.js"></script>
<script src="js/apps/contacts/app.js"></script>
<script type="text/javascript">App.start();</script>
```

This is the standard way of script loading; the browser is responsible to parse these script tags, fetch the script files from the assets server, and then execute them in that order. So that the Browser will execute jQuery, then Bootstrap, then Underscore and so on.

As you know, Backbone depends on Underscore and jQuery to work; it uses jQuery to handle DOM selections in Backbone views and Underscore as the utility library. For this reason, jQuery and Underscore should be loaded before Backbone.

In the project code, app.js depends on Backbone, so that it's loaded after Backbone. The apps/contacts/app.js module is the application façade. It depends on all the other modules in the subapplications, which is why it's loaded last.

Figure 4.2 shows the dependency of the modules graphically. Note that it's a simplification and not all the dependencies are shown.

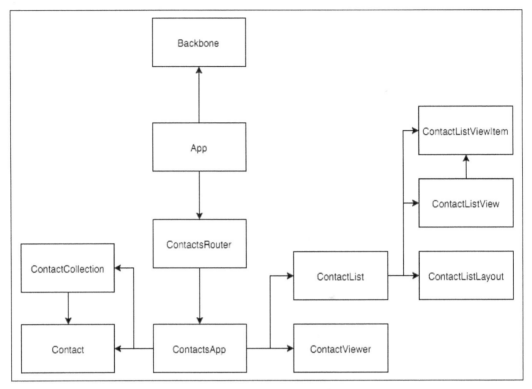

Figure 4.2 Dependency graph

Using Browserify in the app

Until now we have learned about what Browserify is and how to use it. Now we will apply that background to our contacts app to load all the code as Node modules.

Before we continue, ensure that you have installed all the required dependencies for the project:

```
{
  "name": "mastering-backbone-04",
  // ...
  "dependencies": {
    "backbone": "^1.2.3",
    "backbone-validation": "^0.11.5",
    "body-parser": "^1.14.1",
    "bootstrap": "^3.3.5",
```

```
        "browser-sync": "^2.9.11",
        "crispy-string": "0.0.2",
        "express": "^4.13.3",
        "http-proxy": "^1.11.3",
        "jquery": "^2.1.4",
        "lodash": "^3.10.1",
        "morgan": "^1.6.1",
        "sweetalert": "^1.1.3",
        "underscore": "^1.8.3"
    }
}
```

The easiest modules to convert are Models and Collections because they don't have huge dependencies.

```
// apps/contacts/models/contact.js
'use strict'

var Backbone = require('backbone');

class Contact extends Backbone.Model {
  // ...
}


module.exports = Contact;
```

As you can see, the module remains almost the same. We have just added the require() calls and the export statement at the end of the file:

```
// apps/contacts/contactCollection.js
'use strict';

var Backbone = require('backbone');
var Contact = require('../models/contact');

class ContactCollection extends Backbone.Collection {
  // ...

  get model() {
return Contact;
  }
}


module.exports = ContactCollection;
```

Views are easy to convert, too. We just have to add the `require()` calls as we did with the `Contact` and `ContactCollection` modules. Before we continue, we need an extra step with the views; currently all the views for a given controller are contained in a single script; `contactEditor.js` for example contains `ContactForm`, `ContactPreview`, and `PhoneList`, and so on.

As we are modularizing the project, it's a good idea to put each view in its own file and require it when we need it. The following shows this idea. You have many good reasons to do this: to isolate your components for testing, to keep your files small, to improve maintenance, and to get interchangeable modules.

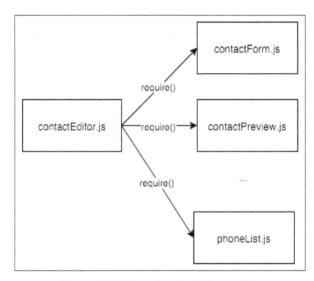

Figure 4.3 Splitting views to their own files

```
'use strict';

var Layout = require('../../common').Layout;

class ContactFormLayout extends Layout {
// ...
}

module.exports = ContactFormLayout;
```

As you can see, the conversion of plain JavaScript files to Node modules is very easy to do. The code of the business logic is exactly the same. The subapplication controller depends on the views that we have converted on the previous step.

```
'use strict';

var _ = require('underscore');
var Backbone = require('backbone');
var App = require('../../app');
var ContactFormLayout = require('./views/contactFormLayout');
var ContactPreview = require('./views/contactPreview');
var PhoneListView = require('./views/phoneListView');
var EmailListView = require('./views/emailListView');
var ContactForm = require('./views/contactForm');
var PhoneCollection = require('./collections/phoneCollection');
var EmailCollection = require('./collections/emailCollection');

class ContactEditor {
  // ...
}

module.exports = ContactEditor;
```

The application façade depends on many subapplication controllers, the models, and the collections:

```
'use strict';

var App = require('../../app');
var ContactList = require('./contactList');
var ContactViewer = require('./contactViewer');
var ContactEditor = require('./contactEditor');
var Contact = require('./models/contact');
var ContactCollection = require('./collections/contactCollection');

function ContactsApp(options) {
  // ...
}

// ...

module.exports = ContactsApp;
```

The routers depend on the subapplication façade and the application infrastructure:

```
'use strict';

var Backbone = require('backbone');
var App = require('../../app');
var ContactsApp = require('./app');

var ContactsRouter = Backbone.Router.extend({
  // ...
});

module.exports = new ContactsRouter();
```

The App object is responsible for loading all the subapplication routers and then starting the history module:

```
'use strict';

var _ = require('underscore');
var Backbone = require('backbone');
var BackboneValidation = require('backbone-validation');
var swal = require('sweetalert');
var noty = require('noty');
var Region = require('./common').Region;

// Initialize all available routes
require('./apps/contacts/router');

var App = {
start() {
    // The common place where sub-applications will be showed
    App.mainRegion = new Region({el: '#main'});

    // Create a global router to enable sub-applications to
    // redirect to other URLs
    App.router = new DefaultRouter();
    Backbone.history.start();
  },

// ...
};

// ...

module.exports = App;
```

The next step is to start the application by calling the `start()` method on the App object; this is done from the `index.html` file:

```
<script type="text/javascript">App.start();</script>
```

As we are re-packing the application with Browserify, it's better to create a new file to the main entry point:

```
// main.js
var App = require('./app');

App.start();
```

Once our application is written as Node modules, we can use Browserify to bundle the code in a single script:

```
$ mkdir -p .tmp/js
$ cd app/js
$ browserify main.js -o ../../.tmp/js/app.js
```

This will create a bundled file with all the dependencies on it. To use the bundled version of the code, we have to change the `index.htm` file to load it instead of loading all the individual files:

```
<html>
<head>
    // ...
</head>
<body>
// ...
<script src="js/app.js"></script>
</body>
</html>
```

That should be enough; however, the application won't start because we have a cyclic dependency issue.

Solving cyclic dependency

Having two modules that depend on each other is called **cyclic dependency**. In our Contacts application, the infrastructure application depends on the subapplication routers, and the routers depend on the application infrastructure to load the subapplication controllers and facades. Figure 4.4 shows how this looks.

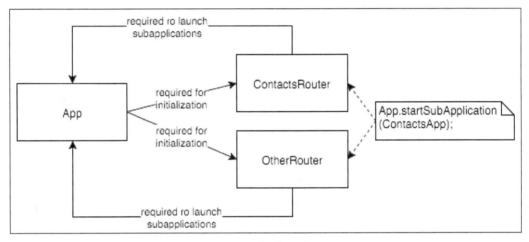

Figure 4.4 Cyclic dependencies

It is not possible to run the application properly because of the cyclic dependency. Here is what happens in detail.

* The App module is executed

* The App requires `ContactsRouter`:

  ```
  var ContactsRouter = require('./apps/contacts/router');
  ```

* `ContactsRouter` requires the App module but the App module is not exported yet:

  ```
  var App = require('../../app'); // returns undefined
  ```

* `ContactsRouter` receives an `undefined` value for the App variable

* The App module continue the execution and finally exposes the App value:

  ```
  var App = {
    // ...
  };

  module.exports = App;
  ```

- `ContactsRouter` matches a route, but as the App value is undefined it triggers an error:

```
startApp() {
  // App = undefined
  return App.startSubApplication(ContactsApp);
}
```

We should break the cycle in some way. An easy approach to do it is to require the App module after it is exported. Instead of requiring the `App` module from `ContactsRouter` on top of the file, we can do it only when it's necessary:

```
// apps/contacts/router.js
class ContactsRouter extends Backbone.Router {
  // ...

  startApp() {
    var App = require('../../app');
    var ContactsApp = require('./app');
    return App.startSubApplication(ContactsApp);
  }
}
```

This is a simple but effective way to break a cyclic dependency. Now you can re-bundle the application and run the application again. It should work:

```
$ mkdir -p .tmp/js
$ cd app/js
$ browserify main.js -o ../../.tmp/js/app.js
```

Modularizing templates

Until now, templates have been declared as script tags in the `index.html` file. While this is a good approach for small projects, it is not a good idea to put all your templates directly in the HTML file.

With Browserify, you can extract all your template files into individual files, with the advantage of modularization and a cleaner `index.html` file. Another benefit of modularizing templates is that you can pre-compile all the templates, saving resources in your users' browsers.

With Browserify, you can modularize almost any template format: jade, Handlebars, Underscore, and so on. It uses a transformation process described in Figure 4.5. If you have worked with other bundler tools such as webpack, transformations are analogous to pre-processors.

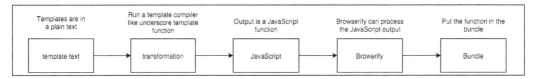

Figure 4.5 The transformation process

Templates are in plain text; the text is passed to a function that compiles it into a JavaScript function that Browserify can process as a regular JavaScript file. To apply the necessary transformation to the templates, you will need to install a transformation plugin:

```
$ npm install --save-dev jstify
```

The transformation process take place when you instruct webpack to use jstify at compilation time:

```
$ browserify main.js -t [ jstify --engine underscore ] -o ../../.tmp/js/app.js
```

Templates are easy to modularize; just extract the text in the script tags and put it in a new file:

```
// apps/contacts/templates/contactListLayout.tpl
<div class="actions-bar-container"></div>
<div class="list-container"></div>
<div class="footer text-muted">
  © 2015. <a href="#">Mastering Backbone.js</a> by <a href="https://
twitter.com/abieealejandro" target="_blank">Abiee Alejandro</a>
</div>
```

The contactListLayout.tpl now contains the text of the layout template for the contact list. In the ContactListLayout view you can import the template as a regular JavaScript file but do not forget to include the tpl extension:

```
// apps/contacts/views/contactListLayout.js
'use strict';

var Layout = require('../../../common').Layout;
var template = require('../templates/contactListLayout.tpl');

class ContactListLayout extends Layout {
```

```
  constructor(options) {
    super(options);
    this.template = template;
    this.regions = {
      actions: '.actions-bar-container',
      list: '.list-container'
    };
  }

  get className() {
    return 'row page-container';
  }
}


module.exports = ContactListLayout;
```

When you import the template, you will use a function. Because our common views support both CSS selectors and pre-compiled templates it should work properly:

```
// common.js
render() {
  // Get JSON representation of the model
  var data = this.serializeData();
  var renderedHtml;

  // If template is a function assume that is a compiled
  // template, if not assume that is a CSS selector where
  // the template is defined and is compatible with
  // underscore templates
  if (_.isFunction(this.template)) {
    renderedHtml = this.template(data);
  } else if (_.isString(this.template)) {
    var compiledTemplate = this.compileTemplate();
    renderedHtml = compiledTemplate(data);
  }

  this.$el.html(renderedHtml);

  // Call onRender callback if is available
  if (this.onRender) {
    this.onRender();
  }

  return this;
}
```

Now you have a fully modularized project where each piece of code is in a small file; one advantage of this is that you can focus on small chunks of code instead and avoid the overhead of large files.

Summary

In this chapter, we have learned what Browserify is and how you can organize your projects into Node modules to manage your code and dependencies in a cleaner way. To make the Contacts project compatible with npm, we had to alter the code of the project; however, the changes are minimal.

There are other alternatives to Browserify, too; require.js and the AMD module definition are good to work with. However testing with require.js could be very difficult; I don't recommend you use require.js if you want to test isolated modules (unit testing).

Webpack is another popular choice to bundle and organize your code base. Its main purpose is to work with frontend dependencies; it can load CommonJS modules and AMD modules. However, webpack is more complicated to configure and manage.

Browserify is the most popular choice for bundling JavaScript projects and is easier to configure and maintain than webpack; it is useful to use the same tools that Node uses to manage its dependencies and it does a great job.

In the next chapter, we will explore how to deal with files in a Backbone project; handling files over a RESTful API is a common issue, so we will discover what the common patterns and strategies are.

In Chapter 7, we will explore how to build applications with automation tools; instead of manually running the Browserify command each time we change the code, we will create the necessary scripts that will do it for us.

5
Dealing with Files

When you are building a Backbone application you will consume resources from a RESTful web service; however most of the RESTful services use the JSON format to encode information, but JSON is not suitable to send and receive files. How we can send files to a RESTful server?

If you are developing an application that is not JavaScript–intensive, you can send files through an HTML form, but in **Single Page Applications (SPA)** this is not the best way to do it. Another issue is that Backbone does not provide an easy mechanism to send files because it is not compatible with the RESTful specification.

But web applications need to work with files. There are some approaches to deal with this common issue. For example, you could use a traditional POST form on resources where files may be included; however, that's not a good option. In this chapter you will learn the following:

- Handle file uploads from an Express server
- Adopt strategies to send files to a RESTful server
- Upload files
- Create a resource that includes a file in it

We will start by adding support for uploading files to an Express server because it is important to know how a server can respond to upload requests.

Express server

To demonstrate how to send files to a server, in this chapter we will work with the latest version of Express (the latest version available at the time of writing is Express 4.x). The server will be responsible for storing the REST resources and handling file uploads. Please consult the GitHub repo for this book to get the implementation of the server for the previous chapters.

For now, the current server is able to create, get, update, and delete contact resources; we need to add a mechanism to upload an avatar image for a contact. For simplicity the application does not use a database to store its data, but instead uses a hash table to store all data in memory. For example, the next snippet demonstrates how to store a contact:

```
// Insert a new contact JSON into the contacts array
createContact(req, res) {
var contact = extractContactData(req);

  // Asssign a random id
  contact.id = makeId();
contacts.push(contact);

res.status(201)
.json(contact);
}
```

Attaching a file into a resource

Before we start receiving files in the Express server, we need to set up a strategy for that. We still want to use the RESTful services, so changing the format of the transmission data is not an option.

Respecting the RESTful standard (for more on the REST design for file uploads, see `http://bit.ly/1GXqPNY`), we can attach a subresource endpoint under the target resource to handle the uploads, so that it will not disturb the original resource. However, this approach has a limitation: the resource should exist first, which means that you cannot create a contact and its avatar photo at the same time.

Following this approach, the endpoint for the avatar file uploading can be located at:

```
http://example.com/api/contacts/10/avatar
```

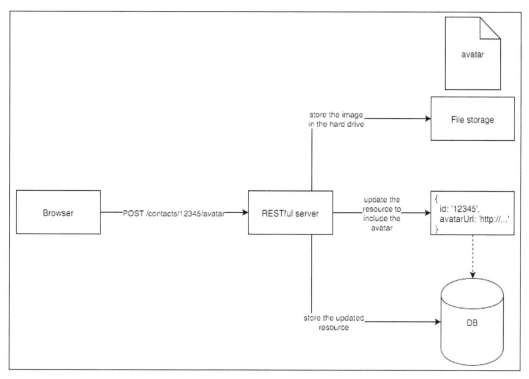

Figure 5.1 File uploading schema

The preceding figure shows the schema for how file uploading should be handled by the server; the avatar endpoint will handle POST requests encoded as `multipart/form-data` instead of JSON, because that's the only way to upload files using the HTTP protocol. Note that in the endpoint it's included the contact id; in this way, once the file is uploaded we can associate the file with the resource. Though the endpoint does not accept a JSON as input, it can return a JSON to inform about the process:

```
{
    "success": true,
    "avatar": {
      "file": "something.jpg",
      "url": "http://example.com/avatar/something.jpg"
    }
}
```

In this example result, the server is telling us that we can access the avatar through the `http://example.com/avatar/something.jpg` URL. We need to modify the contact resource to include this new information in it:

```
{
  "name": "John Doe",
  "email": "john.doe@example.com",
"avatar": {
    "file": "something.jpg",
    "url": "http://example.com/avatar/something.jpg"
  }

}
```

The contact resource now includes the avatar information so that it can be used to show the avatar wherever it's needed — for example, in the contact list. To display the avatar image, the only thing you need to do is include the avatar URL in an `img` tag.

The server should be able serve these files too. In the simplest workflow, you can put all the avatar images in a common path and serve that path as regular assets; the downside of this approach is that anyone can see the files if they have the name of the file.

Uploading the avatar photo to contacts

Let's start by creating the endpoint to upload avatar photos:

```
// routes.js
var controller = require('./controller');

//...
server.post('/api/contacts/:contactId/avatar',
controller.uploadAvatar);
```

Express itself does not process files automatically; it needs a plug-in that transforms the raw request into a more user-friendly API. This plug-in is named `multer`; it processes `multipart/form-data`, saving the file into a temporary path or making a buffer object, and then provides a JSON object with metadata information:

```
// Avatar endpoints
var upload = multer();
server.post('/api/contacts/:contactId/avatar', upload.
single('avatar'),
controller.uploadAvatar
);
server.use('/avatar', express.static(__dirname + '/avatar'));
```

With the default configuration, it will save all the uploaded files into the temporary path of your operating system, which is /tmp in Unix systems; multer will attach a files attribute in the req object, which we can inspect to retrieve information about the uploaded files:

```
uploadAvatar(req, res, next) {
varcontactId = req.params.contactId;
var filename, fullpath;

  // Ensure that user has sent the file
  if (!_.has(req, 'file')) {
    return res.status(400).json({
      error: 'Please upload a file in the avatar field'
    });
  }

  // File should be in a valid format
var metadata = req.file;
  if (!isValidImage(metadata.mimetype)) {
res.status(400).json({
      error: 'Invalid format, please use jpg, png or gif files'
    });
    return next();
  }

  // Get target contact from database
var contact = _.find(contacts, 'id', contactId);
  if (!contact) {
res.status(404).json({
      error: 'contact not found'
    });
    return next();
  }

  // Ensure that avatar path exists
  if (!fs.existsSync(AVATAR_PATH)) {
fs.mkdirSync(AVATAR_PATH);
  }

  // Ensure unique filename to prevent name colisions
var extension = getExtension(metadata.originalname);
  do {
    filename = generateFilename(25, extension);
fullpath = generateFullPath(filename);
```

```
    } while(fs.existsSync(fullpath));

    // Remove previous avatar if any
    removeAvatar(contact);

    // Save the file in disk
    varwstream = fs.createWriteStream(fullpath);
    wstream.write(metadata.buffer);
    wstream.end();

    // Update contact by assingn the url of the uploaded file
    contact.avatar = {
        file: filename,
    url: generateURLForAvatar(filename)
      };

    res.json({
        success: true,
        avatar: contact.avatar
      });
    }
```

In the first steps, we validate that user has been uploaded a valid file and then we get the target user from the database and, if doesn't exist, we return an Http 404 error. The `multer` plug-in stores the uploaded file in memory, and can be processed before saving the file to the final path; for example, maybe we want to generate a thumbnail file or process the image to save space on disk.

We ensure that the avatar path exists; if doesn't we then create the path. In the next steps, we generate a filename to be assigned to the uploaded file in order to prevent filename collisions; the `generateFilename()` function generates that filename and then checks if it already exists; if it does, then we generate another filename and so on.

Once we have a unique filename for the uploaded file, we store the file from the in-memory buffer to the generated path. Now that the file is in the avatar path, we can build the URL where we can get the image from the browser, and finally assign the URL to the `avatar` field in the contact resource.

Showing the avatar

Now that we can upload images and the contact resource has the information about where the avatar is located, we can show the avatar in our views by pointing an `img` tag to the `avatar.url` property in the `Contact` model:

```
<% if (avatar && avatar.url) { %>
<imgsrc="<%= avatar.url %>" alt="Contact photo" />
<% } else { %>
<imgsrc="http://placehold.it/250x250" alt="Contact photo" />
<% } %>
```

This will show the image, if any; otherwise it will show a default one. We should modify the Contact model to include a default avatar:

```
// apps/contacts/models/contact.js
'use strict';

var Backbone = require('backbone');

class Contact extends Backbone.Model {
// ...

  get defaults() {
    return {
      name: '',
      phone: '',
      email: '',
      address1: '',
      address2: '',
facebook: '',
      twitter: '',
      google: '',
github: '',
      avatar: null
    };
  }

// ...
}

module.exports = Contact;
```

If no avatar image is retrieved from the server, then we use a null image. The following screenshot shows how it looks like when you upload an image. This is enough to show an avatar image where it's necessary. It is very easy to show images. In the rest of the chapter, we will see how to perform the upload:

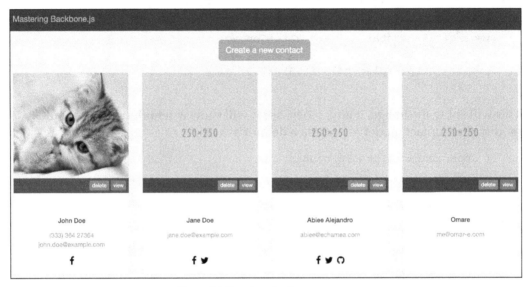

Figure 5.2 Showing the Contact avatar

Uploading images from Backbone

To allow us to upload files from our Backbone application, we should create an input file to be able to show a **Choose** file dialog. This could be done in the `ContactEditor` sub-application by changing the `ContactPreview` class to add this functionality. So let's change the current template and add the input:

```
<div class="box thumbnail">
<div class="photo">
<% if (avatar && avatar.url) { %>
<imgsrc="<%= avatar.url %>" alt="Contact photo" />
<% } else { %>
<imgsrc="http://placehold.it/250x250" alt="Contact photo" />
<% } %>
<input id="avatar" name="avatar" type="file"
style="display: none" />
</div>
<!-- ... -->
</div>
```

Note that we have created a hidden input file field; we don't want to show the input field, but we want the control to open a **Select File** dialog. As the input is hidden, when the user clicks on the current image, we will show the file chooser:

```
// apps/contacts/views/contactPreview.js
class ContactPreview extends ModelView {
// ...

  get events() {
    return {
      'click img': 'showSelectFileDialog'
    };
  }

showSelectFileDialog() {
    $('#avatar').trigger('click');
  }

  // ...
}
```

When the user clicks on the image, it triggers a click event on the input; this will open the **Open file** dialog and allow the user to select a file from his/her hard drive. After the user selects the file, the browser triggers a change event on the file input that we can use to process the selection:

```
// apps/contacts/views/contactPreview.js
class ContactPreview extends ModelView {
// ...

  get events() {
    return {
      'click img': 'showSelectFileDialog',
'change #avatar': 'fileSelected'
    };
  }

  // ...
}
```

The change event will call the fileSelected() method that is responsible for processing the selected file. As we have seen in *Chapter 1, Architecture of a Backbone application* views should not talk to the server directly; for this reason, the view should not make any AJAX calls.

The best place to upload the image is in the Contact model, so the view should only get the selected file and delegate this process to the controller:

```
// apps/contacts/views/contactPreview.js
class ContactPreview extends ModelView {
  // ...

  fileSelected(event) {
  event.preventDefault();

  var $img = this.$('img');

    // Get a blob instance of the file selected
  var $fileInput = this.$('#avatar')[0];
  varfileBlob = $fileInput.files[0];

    // Render the image selected in the img tag
  varfileReader = new FileReader();
  fileReader.onload = event => {
      $img.attr('src', event.target.result);

      // Set the avatar attribute only if the
      // model is new
      if (this.model.isNew()) {
  this.model.set({
          avatar: {
  url: event.target.result
          }
        });
      }
    };
  fileReader.readAsDataURL(fileBlob);

  this.trigger('avatar:selected', fileBlob);
  }
}
```

When a file is selected, we create a `blob` object and trigger an event with the object attached to be processed by the controller. Note that we use the HTML 5 API to immediately show the selected image as the avatar preview:

```
// apps/contacts/contactEditor.js
class ContactEditor {
```

```
// ...

showEditor(contact) {
    // ...

this.listenTo(contactPreview, 'avatar:selected', blob => {
this.uploadAvatar(contact, blob);
    });
  }
}
```

The `uploadAvatar()` method takes a file blob as argument and delegates the server connection to the `Contact` model:

```
// apps/contacts/contactEditor.js
class ContactEditor {
// ...

uploadAvatar(contact, blob) {
    // Tell to others that upload will start
this.trigger('avatar:uploading:start');

contact.uploadAvatar(blob, {
        progress: (length, uploaded, percent) => {
          // Tell to others that upload is in progress
this.trigger('avatar:uploading:progress',
                      length, uploaded, percent);
        },
        success: () => {
          // Tell to others that upload was done successfully
this.trigger('avatar:uploading:done');
        },
        error: err => {
          // Tell to others that upload was error
this.trigger('avatar:uploading:error', err);
        }
    });
  }
}
```

The controller will trigger `'avatar:uploading:*'` events to reflect the status of the uploading process. These events can be listened for the view to give visual feedback to the user. Figure 5.3 graphically shows the communication between the controller and the view:

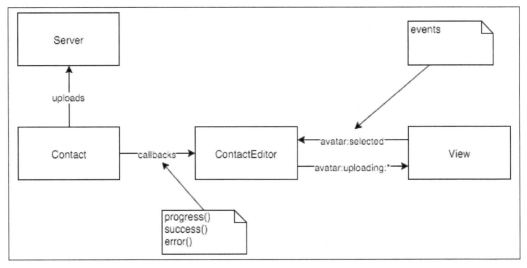

Figure 5.3 Event communication between the view and controller

The `uploadEvent()` method in the Contact model accepts a blob object as the first argument, which is the file that will be uploaded, and an `options` object with three possible functions that will be called as the communication with the server proceeds.

As you may guess, `success` and `error` callbacks will be called if the server accepts the file or if a error happens, respectively. Large files are divided and uploaded to the server in chunks; the `progress()` callback is called as the chunks are received in the server. With the information provided in the `progress()` handler, we can update a progress bar to show the progress to the user:

```
// apps/contacts/views/contactPreview.js
class ContactPreview extends ModelView {
  constructor(options) {
    super(options);
this.template = template;

this.model.on('change', this.render, this);

    if (options.controller) {
this.listenTo(
options.controller, 'avatar:uploading:start',
this.uploadingAvatarStart, this
```

```
        );
this.listenTo(
options.controller, 'avatar:uploading:done',
this.uploadingAvatarDone, this
        );
this.listenTo(
options.controller, 'avatar:uploading:error',
this.uploadingAvatarError, this
        );
    }
  }

uploadingAvatarStart() {
this.originalAvatarMessage = this.$('span.info').html();
this.$('span.notice').html('Uploading avatar...');
    }

uploadingAvatarDone() {
this.$('span.notice').html(this.originalAvatarMessage || '');
    }

uploadingAvatarError() {
this.$('span.notice').html(
'Can\'t upload image, try again later'
);
    }
  }
```

As the events are triggered by the controller, the view updates the message displayed to the user, so that the user can see if an error occurs, or supplies an uploading message to show what the application is doing.

We should pass the controller instance to the view at creation time:

```
class ContactEditor {
// ...

showEditor(contact) {
    // ...
varcontactPreview = new ContactPreview({
    controller: this,
    model: contact
  });
  }
}
```

Uploading a file with AJAX

The `Client` model receive the blob object, builds the URL to the `avatar` endpoint, and makes the appropriate calls to the callback objects:

```
// apps/contacts/models/contact.js
class Contact extends Backbone.Model {
  // ...

uploadAvatar(imageBlob, options) {
    // Create a form object to emulate a multipart/form-data
varformData = new FormData();
formData.append('avatar', imageBlob);

varajaxOptions = {
url: '/api/contacts/' + this.get('id') + '/avatar',
      type: 'POST',
      data: formData,
      cache: false,
contentType: false,
processData: false
    };

    options = options || {};

    // Copy options to ajaxOptions
_.extend(ajaxOptions, _.pick(options, 'success', 'error'));

    // Attach a progress handler only if is defined
    if (options.progress) {
ajaxOptions.xhr = function() {
varxhr = $.ajaxSettings.xhr();

        if (xhr.upload) {
           // For handling the progress of the upload
xhr.upload.addEventListener('progress', event => {
            let length = event.total;
            let uploaded = event.loaded;
            let percent = uploaded / length;

options.progress(length, uploaded, percent);
          }, false);
        }

        return xhr;
```

```
    };
  }

$.ajax(ajaxOptions);
  }

  // ...
}
```

See how the model builds the endpoint from its own data so that the view is decoupled of any server connection. As the `multipart/form-data POST` is not managed natively by the browser, we should create a `FormData` object that represents a form data structure, and add an `avatar` field (the field name that is expecting the server).

They key attribute in the `$.ajax()` call is `processData`, which is set to `false`; you can read the following in the jQuery documentation:

By default, data passed in to the data option as an object (technically, anything other than a string) will be processed and transformed into a query string, fitting to the default content-type "application/x-www-form-urlencoded". If you want to send a DOMDocument, or other non-processed data, set this option to false.

If you don't set this attribute to `false`, or leave it at the default, jQuery will try transform the `formData` object and the file will not be sent.

If a progress attribute is set in the `options` object, we overwrite the original `xhr()` function called by jQuery to get an `XMLHttpRequest` object instance; this allow us to listen for the `progress` event triggered by the browser while uploading the file.

Uploading the avatar image at creation time

As we have seen so far, to upload and attach a file to a resource, it must already exist. How we can create a resource with a file attached? How can we create a contact that includes an avatar image?

To do so, we will need to create the resource in two steps. In the first step, we create the resource itself, and then in a second step we can upload all files we want to that resource. Yes, it's not possible to do this in a single server connection, at least without encoding the files you want to send:

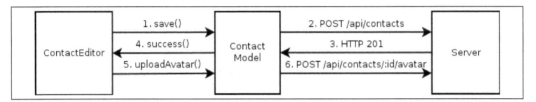

Figure 5.4 Create contact process

The preceding figure shows how the process is done. Note that the model is responsible for handling these connections while the controller orchestrates the order of the communication and error handling. As we have seen previously, the `ContactEditor` triggers several events that the view can use to show to the user what's happening.

The views can be left as is; we should only modify the `ContactEditor` controller by changing how the `saveContact()` method behaves. However, we want to keep the feature of uploading the image as the user makes the selection. If the Contact model is new, this feature will break the application because no valid endpoint exists to upload the avatar:

```
class ContactEditor {
// ...

showEditor(contact) {
    // ...

    // When avatar is selected, we can save it inmediatly if the
    // contact already exists on the server, otherwise just
    // remember the file selected
this.listenTo(contactPreview, 'avatar:selected', blob => {
this.avatarSelected = blob;

    if (!contact.isNew()) {
this.uploadAvatar(contact);
    }
    });
}
}
```

When an avatar is selected, instead of immediately uploading the file to the server, we check if the contact is new or not. If the model is not new, we can perform the upload by calling the `uploadAvatar()` method; otherwise, we keep a reference to the blob object in the `avatarSelected` attribute that the `uploadAvatar()` method will use when it is called.

The `saveContact()` method is responsible for orchestrating the algorithm described in the previous figure:

```
// apps/contacts/contactEditor.js
class ContactEditor {
saveContact(contact) {
varphonesData = this.phones.toJSON();
varemailsData = this.emails.toJSON();

contact.set({
    phones: phonesData,
    emails: emailsData
  });

    if (!contact.isValid(true)) {
      return;
    }

varwasNew = contact.isNew();

    // The avatar attribute is read-only
    if (contact.has('avatar')) {
contact.unset('avatar');
    }

    function notifyAndRedirect() {
      // Redirect user to contact list after save
App.notifySuccess('Contact saved');
App.router.navigate('contacts', true);
    }

contact.save(null, {
    success: () =>{
      // If we are not creating an user it's done
      if (!wasNew) {
notifyAndRedirect();
```

```
        return;
    }

    // On user creation send the avatar to the server too
this.uploadAvatar(contact, {
        success: notifyAndRedirect
    });
  },
error() {
        // Show error message if something goes wrong
App.notifyError('Something goes wrong');
      }
    });
  }
  // ...
}
```

Before calling the save() method in the Contact model, it's necessary to save whether the model is new or not; if we call this method after the save, the isNew() method will always return true.

If the model wasn't new, then any changes in the avatar image were already uploaded by the 'avatar:selected' event handler, so we don't need to upload the image again. But if the image was new, then we should upload the avatar by calling the uploadAvatar() method; note that the method accepts an options object to register callbacks. This is necessary to provide feedback to the user; when the upload is done it calls the notifyAndRedirect() function to show a notification message and returns to the list of contacts.

We will need to change the implementation of uploadAvatar() to include the callbacks described earlier and to instead receive the blob as soon as it uses the avatarSelected attribute:

```
// apps/contacts/contactEditor.js
uploadAvatar(contact, options) {
  // Tell to others that upload will start
this.trigger('avatar:uploading:start');

contact.uploadAvatar(this.avatarSelected, {
    progress: (length, uploaded, percent) => {
      // Tell to others that upload is in progress
this.trigger('avatar:uploading:progress',
                length, uploaded, percent);
      if (options &&_.isFunction(options.success)) {
options.success();
```

```
      }
    },
    success: () => {
        // Tell to others that upload was done successfully
    this.trigger('avatar:uploading:done');
    },
    error: err => {
        // Tell to others that upload was error
    this.trigger('avatar:uploading:error', err);
    }
  });
}
```

The method is basically the same; we just add the options callbacks and change the source of the blob object.

Encoding the upload file

Another approach to uploading files is to encode the file into base64. When you encode a binary file to base64, the result is a string that we can use as an attribute in the request object.

Though it can be useful to create objects with the file attached in the resource, or to use it as another resource in the server, this is not a recommended approach. This approach has some limitations:

- If the backend server is a node, the thread will be locked until the server decodes the base64 string. This will lead to a low-performance app.
- You cannot upload large amounts of data.
- If the file is large, the Backbone application will freeze until the file is encoded to base64.

If you are uploading very small amounts of data and don't have a huge amount of traffic, you can use this technique; otherwise, I encourage you to avoid it. Instead of uploading the file we can encode it:

```
class ContactEditor {
  // ...

  showEditor(contact) {
      // ...
    this.listenTo(contactPreview, 'avatar:selected', blob => {
    this.setAvatar(contact, blob);
      });
```

```
    }

    setAvatar(contact, blob) {
    varfileReader = new FileReader();

    fileReader.onload = event => {
        let parts = event.target.result.split(',');
    contact.set('avatarImage', parts[1]);
        };

    fileReader.readAsDataURL(blob);
    }
}
```

Of course the server implementation should be able to decode the `avatarImage` and store it as an image file.

Summary

In this chapter, we have seen how to upload files to the server; this is not the only way to do it, but is the more extended and flexible approach. Another possible method is to serialize the image into `base64` in the browser, then set the output string as an attribute in the model; when ten models are saved, the file encoded in `base64` will be part of the payload. The server should decode the string and process the result as a file.

We saw how to decouple the view from the business logic. The view should only process DOM events and trigger business logic level events; then a controller can deal with blob objects instead of low-level DOM nodes. This approach helped us to move upload processing from the view to the model, which is the ideal way to do it.

Finally, we dealt with the creation process; we cannot create a resource and attach files at the same time. We should first create the resource and then send all the files to the server as needed.

In the next chapter, you will learn how to store information directly in the browser. Instead of using a RESTful server, it might be nice to run standalone web applications that don't need a server to run.

6
Store data in the Browser

Backbone was mainly designed to work with RESTful API servers; however, you don't want to always store the data in a server for offline applications or to bust application loading storing cache data in the browser.

We have two choices to store data in the user browser: use localStorage or the new IndexedDB API. While localStorage has wide support on major browsers, IndexedDB is the new specification that is yet to be supported in the near future. Another option that is available currently; however, in deprecated status is Web SQL. If you are developing modern web applications, you should avoid using Web SQL.

In this chapter, you will learn the following topics:

- Basics of localStorage
- Basics of IndexedDB
- Using localStorage instead of a RESTful server to store information
- Using IndexedDB instead of a RESTful server to store information

The localStorage

The localStorage is the simplest and the most supported browser data store. At the moment of writing this book, it is supported in almost all the major browsers. As shown in the figure below, the only browser that does not support localStorage is Opera Mini:

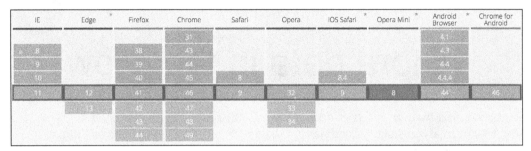

Figure 6.1 Browser support of localStorage

The localStorage is a simple key/value database that is able to only store text. In localStorage, you have three main methods to access the data: `setItem()`, `getItem()`, and `removeItem()`. With these three functions, you can manage the data in the store pretty well.

The downside of localStorage is that it does not have tables or collections, therefore, all the data is mixed; another issue with localStorage is that it is limited to 5 Mb of information. If your storage requirements are bigger than that, you will need IndexedDB.

Starting with localStorage

To store the data in the localStorage store, you need to call the `setItem()` method in the `localStorage` global object:

```
localStorage.setItem('myKey', 'myValue');
localStorage.setItem('name', 'John Doe');
```

That's it, this would store the information in the browser. We can explore the result of these instructions in Google Chrome as seen in the following figure:

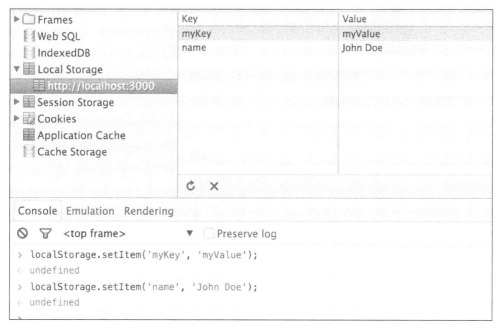

Figure 6.2 Google Chrome and localStorage

The data stored in localStorage is organized by site, which means that can you can only access the data stored on your site. In the above figure, you can see the available sites (`http://localhost:4000`) on the left-hand side. On the right-hand side, you can explore the data that we have stored with the `setItem()` method for the given site.

To retrieve the information from localStorage, you have to use the `getItem()` method:

```
localStorage.getItem('myKey'); // myValue
localStorage.getItem('name'); // John Doe
localStorage.getItem('notExists'); // null
```

To delete an item from the store, we can use the `removeItem()` method:

```
localStorage.removeItem('name');
localStorage.getItem('name'); // null
```

As mentioned earlier, localStorage only stores strings on it. However, we want to store objects, how do we do that?

```
varmyObj = {name: 'John Doe', age: 26};
localStorage.setItem('object', myObj);
localStorage.getItem('object'); // [Object object]
```

Oops…that's not what we expected. The localStorage automatically converts the object into string before storing the object. You can serialize objects with the JSON.stringify() function so that localStorage receives a string instead of an object:

```
varmyObj = {name: 'John Doe', age: 26};
var serialized = JSON.stringify(myObj);

localStorage.setItem('object', serialized);
```

To get the stored object back, you can use the JSON.parse() inverse function that converts a string into an object:

```
var data = localStorage.getItem('object');
varobj = JSON.parse(data);
```

This is how you can store and retrieve objects from localStorage. You will need to encode and decode objects as you go. It is not recommended to store big objects in localStorage due to the heavy use of JSON functions; every time you encode or decode an object, the JavaScript thread will block that object.

Backbone and localStorage

To store Backbone models in localStorage, you can use the ID attribute as key and the serialized data as the value. However, remember that all the data in localStorage is mixed and this strategy will lead to identifier collisions.

Consider that you have two different models (contacts and invoices) with the same ID; when you store one of them in the localStorage, it will overwrite the other.

Another issue with localStorage is that when you want to retrieve data from the store before getting an item from the store, you need to know which key does it have. However, in localStorage, we don't have a clue about what IDs are currently in the store, therefore, we need a way to keep track of the IDs that are in the store at a given time.

To deal with these issues, you can create a well-known key in the store as an index of the IDs that are available for a given collection. See how it works in the following:

```
var data = localStorage.get('contacts'); // index name
varavailableIds = data.split(',');
varcontactList = [];

// Get all contacts
for (leti = 0; i<availableIds.length; i++) {
let id = availableIds[i];
let contact = JSON.parse(localStorage.getItem(id));
contactList.push(contact);
}
```

To prevent collision between collections of models with the same ID, you can generate prefixed keys for the collection items so that instead of having number keys such as 1, you can use keys such as contacts-1:

```
var data = localStorage.get('contacts'); // 1, 5, 6
varavailableIds = data.split(',');
varcontactList = [];

// Get all contacts
for (let i = 0; i<availableIds.length; i++) {
let id = 'contacts-' + availableIds[i];
let contact = JSON.parse(localStorage.getItem(id));
contactList.push(contact);
}
```

Store models in localStorage

Now that you know how to store and retrieve data from localStorage, it's time to store your models. In the following figure, you can see how to make data storage in local instead of a remote server.

By default, when you call the save() method on a model Backbone, it transforms the action into an HTTP request for a RESTFul server. To store the data in local, you need to change the default behavior in order to use localStorage instead of making HTTP requests; you will learn how to do this in the next section.

To make the storage layer maintainable, you will need to create a Backbone driver for localStorage first. The responsibility of the driver is to store and retrieve data from localStorage so that the connection between Backbone and localStorage is simpler:

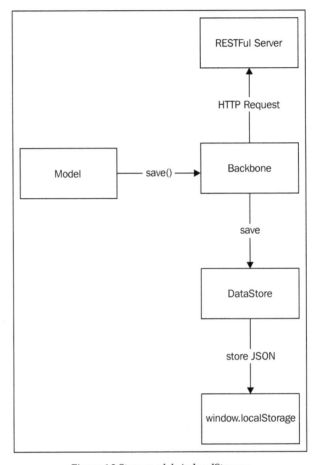

Figure 6.3 Store models in localStorage

In the next section, I will show you how to construct the DataStore driver to store the Backbone models in localStorage.

Store Backbone models in localStorage

It's time to use what you have learned about `localStorage` to store and retrieve objects. The `DataStore` object is responsible to transform models into strings to be stored in localStorage:

```
class DataStore {
  constructor(name) {
    this.name = name;

    // Keep track of all ids stored for a particular collection
this.index = this.getIndex();
  }

getIndex() {
var index = localStorage.getItem(this.name);
    return (index &&index.split(',')) || [];
  }
}
```

The DataStore object needs a name to be used as a collection index prefix. The first use case is to create a new item:

```
class DataStore {
// ...

  create(model) {
    // Assign an id to new models
    if (!model.id&& model.id !== 0) {
      model.id = generateId();
model.set(model.idAttribute, model.id);
    }

    // Save model in the store with an unique name,
    // e.g. collectionName-modelId
localStorage.setItem(
this.itemName(model.id), this.serialize(model)
    );

    // Keep track of stored id
this.index.push(model.get(model.idAttribute));
this.updateIndex();

    // Return stored model
    return this.find(model);
  }
}
```

When a new model is created, it assigns a new ID with a `generateId()` function:

```
var crispy = require('crispy-string');

const ID_LENGTH = 10;

function generateId() {
  return crispy.base32String(ID_LENGTH);
}
```

The `itemName()` function generates a key that is to be used in localStorage given the model ID; the `serialize()` method transforms a model into a JSON string that is ready to be stored in localStorage. Finally, the `index` attribute in DataStore tracks all the available IDs so that we should push the model ID in the index.

For the update method, we will overwrite the current value of the model:

```
class DataStore {
// ...

  update(model) {
      // Overwrite the data stored in the store,
      // actually makes the update
localStorage.setItem(
this.itemName(model.id), this.serialize(model)
      );

      // Keep track of the model id in the collection
varmodelId = model.id.toString();
      if (_.indexOf((this.index, modelId)) >= 0) {
this.index.push(modelId);
this.updateIndex();
      }

      // Return stored model
      return this.find(model);
  }
}
```

If you call the `setItem()` method with an existent key on localStorage, the previous value is overwritten with the new one, the net effect is an update operation.

When you are looking for a model, you need to set the ID of the model and call the fetch() method on it in order to retrieve the data from a server. In our DataStore, we can call this operation find:

```
class DataStore {
// ...

   find(model) {
      return this.deserialize(
localStorage.getItem(this.itemName(model.id))
      );
   }
}
```

The find() method is very simple, it tries to get the data from localStorege with an ID built with the itemName() method; if the model is not found, it will return a null value. While returning a single model is very simple, retrieving a list of them is a more complex operation:

```
class DataStore {
// ...

findAll() {
var result = [];

    // Get all items with the id tracked for the given collection
    for (let i = 0, id, data; i<this.index.length; i++) {
       id = this.index[i];
       data = this.deserialize(localStorage.getItem(
this.itemName(id)
       ));

       if (data) {
result.push(data);
       }
    }

    return result;
   }
}
```

This method loops over all the available keys for the given collection; for each item in the list, it converts it from string to a JSON object. All items are aggregated in a single array that returns as a result.

To remove an item from DataStore, you will need to remove its value from localStorage and drop the index that is related to it:

```
class DataStore {
// ...

  destroy(model) {
      // Remove item from the store
localStorage.removeItem(this.itemName(model.id));

      // Rmoeve id from tracked ids
varmodelId = model.id.toString();
      for (let i = 0; i<this.index.length; i++) {
        if (this.index[i] === modelId) {
this.index.splice(i, 1);
        }
      }
this.updateIndex();

      return model;
  }
}
```

We use the `updateIndex()` method when the collection of models is altered in localStorage; it should store a list of IDs as strings:

```
class DataStore {
// ...

  // Save the ids comma separated for a given collection
updateIndex() {
localStorage.setItem(this.name, this.index.join(','));
  }
}
```

Model IDs are generated with the name of the collection and its ID:

```
class DataStore {
// ...
itemName(id) {
      return this.name + '-' + id;
  }
}
```

The DataStore class, by itself, can store and retrieve models from localStorage; however, it is not fully integrated with Backbone. In the next section, we will examine how Backbone stores and retrieves models from a RESTful API and how to change this behavior to use the DataStore driver.

Backbone.sync

This is responsible to handle connections between a RESTful server and the Backbone application is the Backbone.sync module. It transforms the fetch() and save() operations into HTTP requests:

- fetch() is mapped as a read operation. This will make GET to the the urlRoot attribute with the model ID for a model or the url attribute for a collection.

- save() is mapped as a create or update operation; it depends on the isNew() method:
  - This will be mapped as create if the model does not have an ID (isNew() method return true). A POST request is executed.
  - This will be mapped as update if the model already has an ID (isNew() method returns false). A PUT request is executed.

- destroy() is mapped as a delete operation. This will make DELETE to the the urlRoot attribute with the model ID for a model or the url attribute for a collection.

To better understand how Backbone.sync does its job, consider the following examples:

```
// read operation will issue a GET /contacts/1
varjohn= new Contact({id: 1});
john.fetch();

// update operation will issue a PUT /contacts/1
john.set('name', 'Johnson');
john.save();

// delete operation will issue a DELETE /contacts/1
john.destroy();
varjane = new Contact({name: 'Jane'});
// create operation will issue a POST /contacts
jane.save();
```

As you can read in the Backbone documentation, `Backbone.sync` has the following signature:

```
sync(method, model, [options])
```

Here, the method is the operation that is to be issued (`read`, `create`, `update`, or `delete`). You can easily overwrite this function in order to redirect the requests to localStorage instead of a RESTful server:

```
Backbone.sync = function(method, model, options) {
var response;
var store = model.dataStore ||
                (model.collection&&model.collection.dataStore);
var defer = Backbone.$.Deferred();

  if (store) {
    // Use localstorage in the model to execute the query
    switch(method) {
      case 'read':
        response = model.id ?store.find(model) : store.findAll();
        break;

      case 'create':
        response = store.create(model);
        break;

      case 'update':
        response = store.update(model);
        break;

      case 'delete':
        response = store.destroy(model);
        break;
    }
  }

  // Respond as promise and as options callbacks
  if (response) {
defer.resolve(response);
    if (options &&options.success) {
options.success(response);
    }
  } else {
```

```
defer.reject('Not found');
    if (options &&options.error) {
options.error(response);
    }
  }


  return defer.promise();
};
```

While the localStorage API is synchronous, it does not need to use callbacks or promises; however, in order to be compatible with the default implementation, we need to create a `Deferred` object and return a `promise`.

If you don't know what a promise or `Deferred` objects are, please refer to the jQuery documentation for more information about it. The explanation of how promises work is out of the scope of this book.

The previous `Backbone.sync` implementation is looking for a `dataStore` attribute in the models/collections. The attribute should be included in these objects in order to be stored correctly. As you may guess, it should be an instance of our DataStore driver:

```
// apps/contacts/models/contact.js
class Contact extends Backbone.Model {
  constructor(options) {
    super(options);

this.validation = {
    name: {
      required: true,
minLength: 3
      }
    };

this.dataStore = new DataStore('contacts');
  }
  // ...
}

// apps/contacts/collections/contactCollection.js
class ContactCollection extends Backbone.Collection {
  constructor(options) {
    super(options);
```

```
  this.dataStore = new DataStore('contacts');
    }

  // ...
}
```

The implementation that we made earlier for localStorage is inspired from the Backbone.localStorage plugin. If you want to store all your models in the browser, please use the plugin that has the support of the community.

Due the limitations of localStorage, it is not suitable to store avatar images on it as we will reach the limits with only a few records.

Using localStorage as cache

The Datastore driver is useful to develop small applications that do not need to fetch and store the data in a remote server. It can be enough to prototype small web applications or store configuration data in the browser.

However, another use for the driver can be cache server response in order to speed up the application performance:

```
// cachedSync.js
var _ = require('underscore');
var Backbone = require('backbone');

function getStore(model) {
  return model.dataStore;
}

module.exports = _.wrap(Backbone.sync, (sync, method, model, options)
=> {
var store = getStore(model);

  // Try to read from cache store
  if (method === 'read') {
    let cachedModel = getCachedModel(model);

    if (cachedModel) {
      let defer = Backbone.$.Deferred();
defer.resolve(cachedModel);

      if (options &&options.success) {
options.success(cachedModel);
```

```
    }

        return defer.promise();
    }
  }

    return sync(method, model, options).then((data) => {
      // When getting a collection data is an array, if is a
      // model is a single object. Ensure that data is always
      // an array
      if (!_.isArray(data)) {
        data = [data];
      }

  data.forEach(item => {
        let model = new Backbone.Model(item);
  cacheResponse(method, store, model);
      });
    });
  });
```

When the application needs to read the data, it tries to read the data from localStorage first. If no model is found, it will use the original Backbone.sync function to fetch the data from the server.

When the server responds, it will store the response in localStorage for future use. To cache a server response, it should store the server response or drop the model from the cache when the model is deleted:

```
// cachedSync
function cacheResponse(method, store, model) {
  if (method !== 'delete') {
updateCache(store, model);
  } else {
dropCache(store, model);
  }
}
```

Dropping the model from the cache is quite simple:

```
function dropCache(store, model) {
  // Ignore if cache is not supported for the model
  if (store) {
store.destroy(model);
  }
}
```

To store and retrieve the data in the cache is more complex; you should have a cache expiration policy. For this project, we will expire the cached responses after 15 minutes, which means that we will remove the cached data and then make a `fetch`:

```
// cachedSync.js
// ...

const SECONDS = 1000;
const MINUTES = 60 * SECONDS;
const TTL = 15 * MINUTES;

function cacheExpire(data) {
  if (data &&data.fetchedAt) {
    let now = new Date();
    let fetchedAt = new Date(data.fetchedAt);
    let difference = now.getTime() - fetchedAt.getTime();

    return difference > TTL;
  }

  return false;
}

function getCachedModel(model) {
var store = getStore(model);

  // If model does not support localStorage cache or is a
  // collection
  if (!store&& !model.id) {
    return null;
  }

var data = store.find(model);

  if (cacheExpire(data)) {
dropCache(store, model);
    data = null;
  }

  return data;
}
```

The `fetchedAt` attribute is used to show the time we fetched the data from the server. When the cache expires, it removes the model from the cache and returns `null` to force a server `fetch`.

When a model is cached, it should set the `fetchedAt` attribute for the first time when it is fetched:

```
// cachedSync.js
function updateCache(store, model) {
  // Ignore if cache is not supported for the model
  if (store) {
varcachedModel = store.find(model);

    // Use fetchedAt attribute mdoel is already cached
    if (cachedModel&&cachedModel.fetchedAt) {
model.set('fetchedAt', cachedModel.fetchedAt);
    } else {
model.set('fetchedAt', new Date());
    }

store.update(model);
  }
}
```

Finally, we need to replace the original Backbone.sync function:

```
// app.js
varcachedSync = require('./cachedSync');

// ...

Backbone.sync = cachedSync;
```

IndexedDB

As you have seen in the previous sections, localStorage is very easy; however, it has the limitation of 5 MB of storage capacity. IndexedDB, on the other hand, does not have this limitation; however, it has a complex API. The main downside of IndexedDB is that it is not fully supported on all major browsers:

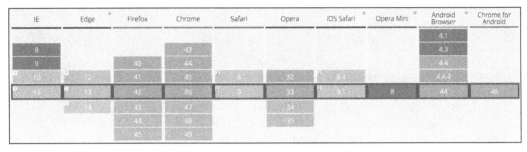

Figure 6.4: Browser support for IndexedDB

At the moment of writing this book, IndexedDB is fully supported by Chrome and Firefox, while Safari and IE have partial support.

A big difference between localStorage and IndexedDB is that IndexedDB is not a key/value store; IndexedDB has collections (tables) and a query API. If you have worked with MongoDB, you will be familiar with the way IndexedDB stores data.

Getting started with IndexedDB

An IndexedDB database is composed of one or more stores. A store is like a JSON container, it contains a collection of JSON. If you have worked with SQL, then a store is like a table. If you have worked with MongoDB, a store is a like a collection. In the same way as MongoDB, IndexedDB is schemaless, which means that you don't need to define the schema of the records (JSONs).

One of the consequences of schemaless is that the data in the collections is not heterogeneous, you can have different types JSON objects in the same store. For example, you can store contact and invoice data in the same store.

IndexedDB is more flexible and powerful than localStorage; however, with great power comes great responsibility. You will have to deal with stores, cursors, indexes, transactions, migrations, and asynchronous API:

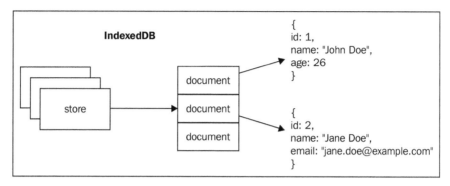

Figure 6.5: IndexedDB

Database versions

Databases usually change with time; maybe a new feature needs a new store or adds an index. All IndexedDB databases have a version number. The first time that you create a new database, it starts with version 1. With the help of each version number, you can define the stores and indexes as you need.

IndexedDB does not allow you to create new stores or indexes, unless you have changed the version number. When a new version number is detected, IndexedDB enters a `versionchange` state and calls the `onupgradedneeded()` callback, which you can use to modify the database.

Every time you change the version number, you have the opportunity to run database migrations in the `onupgradedneeded()` callback. Every time you open a connection with IndexedDB, you can specify a version number:

```
indexedDB.open(<database name>, <version number>)
```

The first time you open a database, IndexedDB enters the `versionchange` state and calls the `onupgradedneeded()` callback.

Creating stores

To create stores on IndexedDB, you need to put the database on the version change state, which you can do in the following two ways:

1. Create a new database.

2. Change the version number of the database.

In the following example, we are creating a new database named library:

```
var request = indexedDB.open("library");

// In this callback the database is in the versionchange state
request.onupgradeneeded = function() {
    // The database did not previously exist, so that
    // we can create object stores and indexes.
vardb = request.result;
var store = db.createObjectStore("books", {keyPath: "isbn"});

    // Populate with initial data.
store.put({
title: "Quarry Memories",
 author: "Fred",
isbn: 123456});
store.put({
title: "Water Buffaloes",
 author: "Fred",
isbn: 234567});
store.put({
title: "Bedrock Nights",
 author: "Barney",
isbn: 345678});
};

request.onsuccess = function() {
window.db = request.result;
};
```

When the open() method is called, it returns a request object that we can use to register the onscuccess() callback called when the database is successfully opened and is ready to be used. As we are creating a new database, the onupgradeneeded() callback is called.

The database handler is in the `result` attribute of the `request` object. You can use the `createObjectStore()` method of the database handler in order to create a new store:

```
createObjectStore(name, options)
```

The first argument of the `createObjectStore()` method is the name of the store, in our example it is library. The `options` arguments should be a plain object where the available fields are as follows:

Option name	Description	Default value
autoIncrement	This auto increments the `primary key` attribute	`false`
keyPath	This is the attribute name in the objects that is to be used as `primary key`	`null`

After the object store creation, a store handler is returned, which you can use to insert new records in the recently created object store. The `put()` method is used to insert new records in the store it accepts as argument the JSON to be stored:

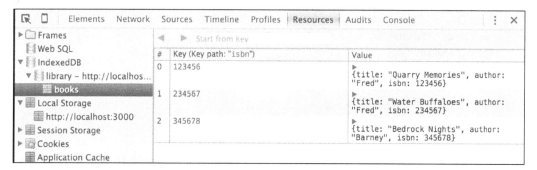

Figure 6.6: IndexedDB in Google Chrome

As you can see in the preceding image, the object store has the objects that we insert with the `put()` method in the `onupgradeneeded` event.

Delete a database

You can always delete a database with the `deleteDatabse()` method. If you did something wrong and want to start over, just delete the database:

```
indexedDB.deleteDatabase('library');
```

Add elements to an object store

You have seen how to create and delete stores. Now, you will see how to connect to a database and add records to an object store outside of the onupgradeneeded() callback:

```
vartx = db.transaction("books", "readwrite");
var store = tx.objectStore("books");

store.put({
  title: "Quarry Memories",
  author: "Fred",
isbn: 123456
});
store.put({
  title: "Water Buffaloes",
  author: "Fred",
isbn: 234567
});
store.put({
  title: "Bedrock Nights",
  author: "Barney",
isbn: 345678
});

tx.oncomplete = function() {
console.log('Records added!');
};
```

Note that we are creating an IndexedDB transaction. The IndexedDB specification by W3C defines a transaction as follows:

A transaction is used to interact with the data in a database. Whenever data is read or written to the database it is done by using a transaction.

Transactions offer some protection from application and system failures. A transaction may be used to store multiple data records or to conditionally modify certain data records. A transaction represents an atomic and durable set of data access and data mutation operations.

The `transaction()` method of the `indexedDB` object has two arguments: scope and mode, as shown in the following table:

Argument	Description	Examples
scope	The store or stores where the transaction interacts	'books', ['contacts', 'invoices']
mode	This states what type of interaction will be done	'readonly', 'readwrite'

When the transaction is created, you can access the stores with the `objectStore()` method of the transaction object, which returns an object store handler that you can use to add or remove records.

The `put()` method is used to insert objects into the store; however, the method is asynchronous, which means that the records are not stored immediately like in localStorage. You should register an `oncomplete()` callback in the transaction object that will be called when the operations are done.

Performing queries

To query the data in an object store, you need to open a `readonly` transaction:

```
vartx = db.transaction("books", "readonly");
var store = tx.objectStore("books");

var request = store.openCursor(IDBKeyRange.only(123456));
request.onsuccess = function() {
var cursor = request.result;
  if (cursor) {
    // Called for each matching record.
console.log(cursor.value);
cursor.continue();
} else {
    // No more matching records, cursor === null
console.log('Done!');
  }
};
```

Queries are to be done by opening cursors with the `openCursor()` method. The first argument of the `openCursor()` method is a query that should be an `IDBKeyRange` object:

- `only(value)`: It looks for the value, such as an == operation
- `lower(value)`: It looks for the values lower or equal to the value, such as a <= operation
- `lowerOpen(value)`: It looks for values lower than the value, such as a < operation
- `upper(value)`: It looks for values greater than or equal to the value, such as a >= operation
- `upperOpen(value)`: It looks for values greater than the value, such as a > operation

These are some of the queries that are available; please refer to the IndexedDB specification for a complete list of all the available queries. IndexedDB uses the query to compare the values that are passed as an argument with the objects in the store; however, which attribute in the store is compared? The answer is the key that is specified in `keyPath`. In our example, the `isbn` attribute will be used.

The cursor will call the `onsuccess()` callback repeatedly for every object found, you should call the `continue()` method on the cursor object to fetch the next object. The result will be `null` when no more objects are found.

If you want to query the objects by a different attribute, you should create indexes in the store for the attributes that you need. Use a different version number to add new indexes to the object stores:

```
var request = indexedDB.open("library", 2);

request.onupgradeneeded = function() {
vardb = request.result;
var store = db.createObjectStore("books", {keyPath: "isbn"});
vartitleIndex = store.createIndex("by_title", "title", {
    unique: true
  });
varauthorIndex = store.createIndex("by_author", "author");

 // ...
};

request.onsuccess = function() {
```

```
db = request.result;

vartx = db.transaction("books", "readonly");
var store = tx.objectStore("books");
var index = store.index("by_title");

var request = index.get("Bedrock Nights");
request.onsuccess = function() {
    // ...
  };
};
```

As you can see in the preceding example, you can use an index to query objects. The same onsuccess() method is invoked every time that the index finds a result.

Delete objects in the store

To delete objects, you should call the delete() method in the object store with a query argument for these objects that you want to remove:

```
vartx = db.transaction("books", "readwrite");
var store = tx.objectStore("books");

store.delete(123456); // deletes book with isbn == 123456
store.delete(IDBKeyRange.lowerBound(456789)); // deletes books with
store <= 456789
```

IndexedDB in Backbone

As the IndexedDB API is more complex than localStorage, it will be more difficult to create an IndexedDB driver for Backbone as we did with localStorage; in this section, you will use what you have learned about IndexedDB in order to build a driver for Backbone.

The driver should open a database and initialize the stores when it is created for the first time:

```
// indexedDB/dataStore.js
'use strict';

var Backbone = require('backbone');

const ID_LENGTH = 10;

var contacts = [
```

```
    // ...
];

class DataStore {
constructor() {
this.databaseName = 'contacts';
  }

openDatabase() {
var defer = Backbone.$.Deferred();

    // If a database connection is already active use it,
    // otherwise open a new connection
    if (this.db) {
defer.resolve(this.db);
    } else {
      let request = indexedDB.open(this.databaseName, 1);

request.onupgradeneeded = () => {
        let db = request.result;
this.createStores(db);
      };

request.onsuccess = () => {
        // Cache recently opened connection
this.db = request.result;
defer.resolve(this.db);
      };
    }

    return defer.promise();
  }

createStores(db) {
var store = db.createObjectStore('contacts', {keyPath: 'id'});

    // Create the first records
contacts.forEach(contact => {
store.put(contact);
    });
  }
}
```

When the connection is opened, it creates the contacts store and puts the first records in the store. After that it caches the database handler in the db attribute to reuse the connection for future requests.

Now, we should create the necessary method to create, update, delete, and read the data from the store:

```
// indexedDB/dataStore.js

var crispy = require('crispy-string');

// ...

class DataStore {
  create(model) {
var defer = Backbone.$.Deferred();

    // Assign an id to new models
    if (!model.id&& model.id !== 0) {
      let id = this.generateId();
model.set(model.idAttribute, id);
    }

    // Get the database connection
this.openDatabase()
.then(db =>this.store(db, model))
.then(result =>defer.resolve(result));

    return defer.promise();
  }

generateId() {
    return crispy.base32String(ID_LENGTH);
  }
  // ...
}
```

When a record is created, we should ensure that the model has an ID. We can generate it for the models that do not have an ID assigned. The store() method will put the record in the indexedDB database:

```
// indexedDB/dataStore.js

var crispy = require('crispy-string');

// ...

class DataStore {
  // ...

store(db, model) {
var defer = Backbone.$.Deferred();

    // Get the name of the object store
varstoreName = model.store;

    // Get the object store handler
vartx = db.transaction(storeName, 'readwrite');
var store = tx.objectStore(storeName);

    // Save the model in the store
varobj = model.toJSON();
store.put(obj);

tx.oncomplete = function() {
defer.resolve(obj);
    };

tx.onerror = function() {
defer.reject(obj);
    };

    return defer.promise();
  }

  // ...
}
```

The `store()` method obtains the name of the store from the `modelstore` attribute and then, creates a `readwrite` transaction for the given store name to put the record on it. The `update()` method uses the same `store()` method to save the record:

```
// indexedDB/dataStore.js
class DataStore {
  // ...

  update(model) {
var defer = Backbone.$.Deferred();

    // Get the database connection
this.openDatabase()
.then(db =>this.store(db, model))
.then(result =>defer.resolve(result));

    return defer.promise();
  }

  // ...
}
```

The update method does not assign an ID to the model, it completely replaces the previous record with the new model data. To delete a record, you can use the `delete()` method of the object store handler:

```
// indexedDB/dataStore.js
class DataStore {
  // ...

destroy(model) {
var defer = Backbone.$.Deferred();

    // Get the database connection
this.openDatabase().then(function(db) {
        // Get the name of the object store
        let storeName = model.store;

        // Get the store handler
vartx = db.transaction(storeName, 'readwrite');
var store = tx.objectStore(storeName);

        // Delete object from the database
```

```
        let obj = model.toJSON();
    store.delete(model.id);

    tx.oncomplete = function() {
    defer.resolve(obj);
        };

    tx.onerror = function() {
    defer.reject(obj);
        };
      });

    return defer.promise();
  }

  // ...
}
```

To get all the models stored on an object store, you need to open a cursor and put all the items in an array, as follows:

```
// indexedDB/dataStore.js
class DataStore {
  // ...

findAll(model) {
var defer = Backbone.$.Deferred();

    // Get the database connection
this.openDatabase().then(db => {
        let result = [];

        // Get the name of the object store
        let storeName = model.store;

        // Get the store handler
        let tx = db.transaction(storeName, 'readonly');
        let store = tx.objectStore(storeName);

        // Open the query cursor
        let request = store.openCursor();

        // onsuccesscallback will be called for each record
        // found for the query
```

```
request.onsuccess = function() {
      let cursor = request.result;

      // Cursor will be null at the end of the cursor
      if (cursor) {
result.push(cursor.value);

          // Go to the next record
cursor.continue();
      } else {
defer.resolve(result);
      }
    };
  });

  return defer.promise();
}

// ...
}
```

Note how this time the transaction opened is in the readonly mode. A single object can be obtained by querying the model ID:

```
// indexedDB/dataStore.js
class DataStore {
  // ...

  find(model) {
var defer = Backbone.$.Deferred();

    // Get the database connection
this.openDatabase().then(db => {
      // Get the name of the collection/store
      let storeName = model.store;

      // Get the store handler
      let tx = db.transaction(storeName, 'readonly');
      let store = tx.objectStore(storeName);

      // Open the query cursor
      let request = store.openCursor(IDBKeyRange.only(model.id));

request.onsuccess = function() {
```

```
        let cursor = request.result;

        // Cursor will be null if record was not found
        if (cursor) {
defer.resolve(cursor.value);
        } else {
defer.reject();
        }
      };
    });

    return defer.promise();
  }

  // ...
}
```

In the same way as we did with localStorage, this IndexedDB driver can be used to overwrite the `Backbone.sync` function:

```
// app.js
var store = new DataStore();

// ...

Backbone.sync = function(method, model, options) {
var response;
var defer = Backbone.$.Deferred();

  switch(method) {
    case 'read':
      if (model.id) {
        response = store.find(model);
      } else {
        response = store.findAll(model);
      }
      break;

    case 'create':
      response = store.create(model);
      break;

    case 'update':
      response = store.update(model);
```

```
        break;

    case 'delete':
        response = store.destroy(model);
        break;
    }

    response.then(function(result) {
        if (options &&options.success) {
    options.success(result);
    defer.resolve(result);
        }
    });

    return defer.promise();
    };
```

Then, models should add the `store` attribute to indicate in which object store the model will be saved:

```
class Contact extends Backbone.Model {
    constructor(options) {
// ,,,
this.store = 'contacts';
    }

    // ...
}

class ContactCollection extends Backbone.Collection {
    constructor(options) {
// ...
this.store = 'contacts';
    }

    // ...
}
```

IndexedDB allows you to store more data than localStorage; therefore, you can use it to store the avatar image too. Just make sure that the avatar attribute is set so that an image is always selected:

```
class ContactPreview extends ModelView {
    // ...

    fileSelected(event) {
    event.preventDefault();

    var $img = this.$('img');

        // Get a blob instance of the file selected
    var $fileInput = this.$('#avatar')[0];
    varfileBlob = $fileInput.files[0];

        // Render the image selected in the img tag
    varfileReader = new FileReader();
    fileReader.onload = event => {
        $img.attr('src', event.target.result);

    this.model.set({
            avatar: {
    url: event.target.result
            }
        });
        };
    fileReader.readAsDataURL(fileBlob);

    this.trigger('avatar:selected', fileBlob);
    }
}
```

Do not try to upload the image:

```
class ContactEditor {
    // ...

    showEditor(contact) {
        // ...

        // When avatar is selected, we can save it inmediatly if the
        // contact already exists on the server, otherwise just
        // remember the file selected
```

```
      //this.listenTo(contactPreview, 'avatar:selected', blob => {
      //   this.avatarSelected = blob;

      //   if (!contact.isNew()) {
      //      this.uploadAvatar(contact);
      //   }
      //});
   }
saveContact(contact) {
// ...

      // The avatar attribute is read-only
      //if (contact.has('avatar')) {
      //   contact.unset('avatar');
      //}

// ...
   }

   // ...
}
```

Summary

You have learned two ways to store data in the browser and use them as a replacement for a RESTful API server. The localStorage method has a simple API and it is widely supported for all major browsers; this is going to be your first choice if you want support old browsers; however, it has the limitation that you can only store five megabytes.

IndexedDB is powerful; however, its API is more complicated than localStorage. You need to learn some concepts before you start working with it. Once you know how it works, you should write your app asynchronously.

7
Build Like a Pro

Some years ago, you could create a website with PHP, upload your source files through FTP to a server, and then go online. During those days, JavaScript was a tight piece of the whole system, used for UI tasks such as validating forms or small chunks of functionality.

Today, web is more JavaScript intensive, we are building web applications instead websites, this means that JavaScript is no more a trivial piece of applications, it is now a core piece. For this reason, it is important to pack our JavaScript application before being deployed for production.

You will learn the following in this chapter:

- Building a workflow to automatically process your source files
- Minifying the application script size
- Minifying the number of requests to the server when the application is loaded
- Minifying the images
- Optimizing the CSS files
- Wiring up everything in an HTML file
- Setting up a development environment to automatically reload the application

At the time of writing this book, there are many tools to build JavaScript applications; however, two of them are the most popular: Grunt and Gulp. Grunt is an older choice with a big community around and an amazing collection of plugins available. Gulp, on the other hand, is gaining more popularity each day and almost has the most popular plugins that exist for Grunt.

Development workflow

When you are developing an application, some tasks are very repetitive; for example, our contacts application uses Browserify to manage dependencies. It needs to rebundle the source code every time you make a change, which means that you need to run the `browserify` command each time:

```
$ npm bundle
```

```
$ npm start
```

To run these commands every time you make a small change is a very tedious task, there should be a better way to do it:

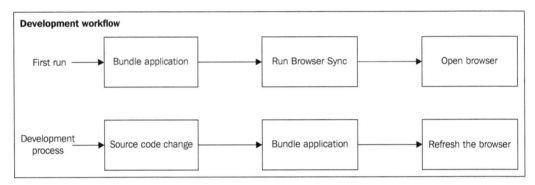

Figure 7.1. Development workflow

The above figure shows the ideal development process; the first time you run the application, you should bundle the source files and run the BrowserSync web server and then open the browser. After that, for any change that you make in any source file, the application should be rebundled and then the browser should be refreshed to get the new changes.

Currently, we are manually doing this process; however, in the next section, you will learn how to automatize this task to let the machine do all this for you.

What's a task runner?

A task runner is computer program that runs a sequence of tasks over your source code, applying transformations to the files. For example, consider that you are writing a source code in the CoffeeScript programming language, one task would be compiling all your source code in JavaScript, other task can be concatenating all the output JavaScript files in a single file, and the third task can finally be minifying the concatenated file to minimize the file size.

These tasks will automatically be run by the task runner, you just need to write a script file to program what needs to be done and then forget to run any command line again. The task runner provides triggers to start a task whenever you change a file so that it is done transparently.

As you can see, a task runner can improve your productivity as you can forget about the details of the compilation process once you have correctly configured a task runner. It will allow you to automate all these repetitive and boring tasks and then, you can focus on product development.

Grunt and Gulp are the most popular task runners for JavaScript; they take different approach to run the tasks. In Grunt, the tasks are run sequentially: once a task is running, the next task cannot start until the first is done. In Gulp, the tasks can run parallel to each other, as shown in the following:

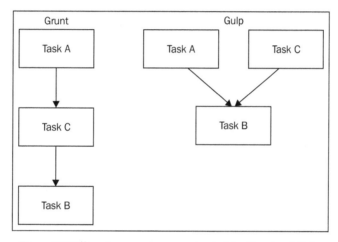

Figure 7.2 Different approach on running task by Grunt and Gulp

The above figure illustrates how Grunt and Gulp will run three tasks. Task B depends on whether Task A and Task C are done. Note that Grunt can run the tasks parallel to each other using plugins. While, Gulp does this from its core design.

Another difference between Grunt and Gulp is that, in Grunt, you can configure the tasks on writing a big configuration object. While, in Gulp, you will write standard JavaScript functions. An interesting point is that Grunt and Gulp can work together in the same project; however, it is better to choose just one of them in order to reduce complexity.

If your project uses Grunt, you should not switch to Gulp unless have a good reason to do it.

How Gulp works

As I mentioned at the beginning of the chapter, Gulp is the most popular JavaScript task runner at the time of writing this book and that's the main reason why we chose it. Gulp and Grunt work in a similar way, they both use third-party plugins to work. Keep in mind that Gulp is more like a framework, it does not make too much by itself.

Gulp acts as the glue that coordinates the build workflow; it has some basic functionality and an API, which the Gulp plugins can use to do their work. The plugins use the compilers and utility programs that make the real file processing, such as the CoffeeScript transpiler. The plugins connect these programs to the Gulp workflow:

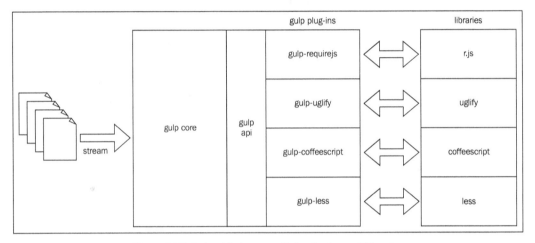

Figure 7.3 Relationship between Gulp plugins and libraries

The preceding figure shows the relationship that was described earlier, you can get a better idea of how Gulp connects with its plugins; notice how the plugins delegate the file processing to the utility programs that they connect to.

Gulp is composed of several named tasks where each task can have dependencies on other tasks. A typical Gulp task opens a stream of files at the beginning and applies transformation to each file in the stream with the installed plugins.

A stream is opened with the `gulp.src()` method. It starts a stream that you can connect to several pipes in order to apply the necessary transformations. When you open a stream, you need to specify the target files that will be used in the stream. You will select these files using the `node-glob format`:

```
// get only the index.html file
gulp.src('app/index.html');

// get all the files with .html extension
gulp.src('app/*.html');

// get all the .js files available 1 path depth in
// the app directory
gulp.src('app/*/*.js');


// get all the .js files in every subdirectory available

gulp.src('app/**/*.js');
```

It is easy to specify the files for the stream, it is similar to what you do in the command line. The figure below shows how the stream and pipes are connected. The files that are selected are streamed into the Gulp plugins, they make the transformations and put the output back in the stream, the next plugin can then make its work, and put the result back in the stream:

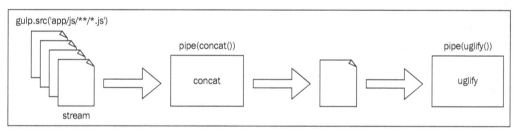

Figure 7.4 Using node-blob to select files

At the end of the pipe, you will normally write the result in a file that is ready to be used. You can put as many Gulp tasks as you need and each task can have as many dependencies as it needs.

Getting started with Gulp

First of all, install the Gulp package globally; this will give you access to the `gulp` command:

```
$ npm install -g gulp
```

Once you have installed Gulp globally, you will need to install it in your local project in order to have access to the Gulp core utilities:

```
$ npm install -save-dev gulp
```

To configure the Gulp tasks, you will need to create a file called `gulpfile.js` that Gulp will read every time you run the `gulp` command. All Gulp tasks have a name and a function that is executed when the task is invoked:

```
var gulp = require('gulp');

gulp.task('hello', function() {
  console.log('Hello world!');
});
```

The following simple Gulp task will print Hello world! on the console:

```
$ gulp hello
[22:43:15] Using gulpfile ~/path/to/project/gulpfile.js
[22:43:15] Starting 'hello'...
Hello world!
[22:43:15] Finished 'hello' after 118 µs
```

Note how we invoke Gulp, `gulp hello`, the argument used in the command is the name of the task to be executed. This is the simplest Gulp task that you can write and it is the starting point for developing an effective build pipeline.

Creating a development workflow

In this section, we will build a script to help us in the development process and, later, to build a production-ready script. You will need to install the basic dependencies first:

```
$ npm install --save-dev gulp gulp-load-plugins gulp-util
```

The `gulp-load-plugins` is useful to automatically load all the available plugins without manually requiring them in the `gulpfile.js` script; the `gulp-util` plugin provides utility functions such as log messages.

Bundling the JavaScript files with Browserify

The `gulp-browserify` plugin is currently deprecated and should not be used. The project author recommends using one of the recipes developed by the Gulp development team.

The recipes described in the repository needs to install some plugins first:

```
$ npm install --save-dev jstifywatchify vinyl-source-stream
```

In `gulpfile.js`, we can define the `browserify` task:

```
var gulp = require('gulp');
var $ = require('gulp-load-plugins')();
var browserify = require('browserify');
var jstify = require('jstify');
var source = require('vinyl-source-stream');

// Bundle files with browserify
gulp.task('browserify', () => {
  // set up the browserify instance on a task basis
  var bundler = browserify({
    entries: 'app/js/main.js',
    debug: true,
    // defining transforms here will avoid crashing your stream
    transform: [jstify]
  });

  return bundler.bundle()
    .on('error', $.util.log)
    .pipe(source('app.js'))
    .pipe(gulp.dest('.tmp/js'));
});
```

Notice how we configure the Browserify bundle, we use the Browserify `jstify` transformation to compile the underscore templates. As the `browserify` task is not a standard Gulp plugin, we are using `vinyl-source-stream` to stream the files to the bundler. Finally, we will write the output in the `.tmp/js` path.

Now, you can run Gulp with the Browserify argument to run the task:

```
$ gulp browserify
[07:13:18] Using gulpfile ~/path/to/your/project/gulpfile.js
[07:13:18] Starting 'browserify'...
[07:13:19] Finished 'browserify' after 1.13 s
```

The `.tmp/js/app.js` file should exist and be ready to be used. You can run the project to verify all is working:

```
$ npm start
```

Sourcemaps

When you run the project, the browser gets a single file named `app.js`, which contains all the concatenated source code. That's good for the production environments as it reduces the number of requests made to the server in order to get the assets. However, in development environments, it is more useful to see the individual files in the browser as you have it in the source code for the debugging process.

You can make sure that the browser shows you the original source files with sourcemaps so that you can put debug breakpoints or simply inspect the code without the noise of the other dependencies such as the Backbone library.

To include sourcemaps in the `browserify` task, you will need to install some extra dependencies:

```
$ npm install --save-dev vinyl-buffergulp-sourcemaps
```

Then, modify the task:

```js
// ...
var buffer = require('vinyl-buffer');

// Bundle files with browserify
gulp.task('browserify', () => {
  // set up the browserify instance on a task basis
  var bundler = browserify({
    entries: 'app/js/main.js',
    debug: true,
    // defining transforms here will avoid crashing your stream
    transform: [jstify]
  });

  return bundler.bundle()
    .on('error', $.util.log)
    .pipe(source('app.js'))
      .pipe(buffer())
      .pipe($.sourcemaps.init({loadMaps: true}))
        // Add transformation tasks to the pipeline here.
        .on('error', $.util.log)
      .pipe($.sourcemaps.write('./'))
    .pipe(gulp.dest('.tmp/js'));
});
```

The following figure shows the source files in the Google Chrome browser. You can inspect the original files and put breakpoints, the browser will ensure to stop the execution at the right time.

It is useful for Browserify bundles to see all the original files instead of a huge script; however, this technique can be used for the compiled programming languages such as CoffeeScript or maybe you can write your source code in ECMAScript 6 and transpile it with babel and then, the original files with sourcemaps:

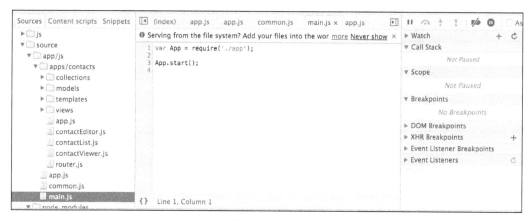

Figure 7.5 Sourcemaps in action

Re-bundle automatically

If you change a source file, then you will need to run the `browserify` task again. You can make sure that Gulp and Browserify do this job for you. First, you will need to install another Browserify plugin:

```
$ npm install --save-dev watchify
```

The `watchify` plugin listens for file changes in the source code and can be used to trigger a re-bundle task:

```
//...
var watchify = require('watchify');

// Bundle files with browserify
gulp.task('browserify-2', () => {
  // set up the browserify instance on a task basis
  var bundler = browserify({
    entries: 'app/js/main.js',
    debug: true,
    // defining transforms here will avoid crashing your stream
    transform: [jstify]
```

```
    });

  bundler = watchify(bundler);

  var rebundle = function() {
    return bundler.bundle()
      .on('error', $.util.log)
      .pipe(source('app.js'))
      .pipe(buffer())
      .pipe($.sourcemaps.init({loadMaps: true}))
        // Add transformation tasks to the pipeline here.
        .on('error', $.util.log)
      .pipe($.sourcemaps.write('./'))
      .pipe(gulp.dest('.tmp/js'));
  };

  bundler.on('update', rebundle);

  return rebundle();
});
```

When a change is triggered, the `rebundle()` function will be executed automatically so that you only need to refresh the browser. In the next section, you will see how to automate this too.

BrowserSync

BrowserSync is an asset server that is useful for the purpose of developing, you should avoid its use for production environments. BrowserSync is a node package that runs an HTTP server that automatically reloads the browser when a change on the files that serve is detected. With BrowserSync, you may forget to manually refresh your browser every time you make a change.

You need to install the package before starting to use it:

```
$ npm install --save-dev browser-sync
```

Once the package is installed, we can create a new Gulp task to run BrowserSync:

```
// ...
var browserSync = require('browser-sync');
var reload = browserSync.reload;

gulp.task('serve', () =>{
  browserSync({
```

```
    port: 9000,
    ui: {
      port: 9001
    },
    server: {
      baseDir: ['.tmp', 'app']
    }
  });

  gulp.watch([
    'app/*.html',
    'app/**/*.css',
    '.tmp/**/*.js'
  ]).on('change', reload);
});
```

On this Gulp task, we will run BrowserSync in the 9000 port and open an additional 9001 port to allow us to configure the BrowserSync behavior. You can, for example, remotely debug your application, which is useful for mobile devices.

We configure BrowserSync to serve the files from the app and .tmp directories. If you access http://localhost:9000/from your browser, the app/index.html file will be served as default and will use the script files in the .tmp directory.

To automatically refresh the browser when a change in the source files is detected, we use the gulp.watch() method as it accepts a list of files to watch in the node-blob format and then, we can listen for the change event to fire a refresh signal to the browser through the reload() function that is included in BrowserSync.

As the server task depends on the availability of the bundle script file, this task should depend on the Browserify task that we earlier created. To indicate Gulp that the task has a dependency, we should add a new argument to the gulp.task() function:

```
// ...
var browserSync = require('browser-sync');
var reload = browserSync.reload;

gulp.task('serve', ['browserify'], () => {
// ...
});
```

The second argument is a list of strings that the task depends on. In the previous snippet, Gulp will ensure that the browserify task runs and finishes first before executing the browserify task function.

Run server with Express

Now that we have the assets server working, we need to run our Express server with `nodemon`, this package is very similar to BrowserSync; however, it does not include the browser features. With nodemon, you can run a node script that will watch for any changes on the JavaScript files. When a change is detected, the node script will be reloaded automatically.

You need to install the npm package first:

```
$ npm install --save-dev gulp-nodemon
```

Then, we can create the task for nodemon:

```
// ...
var nodemon = require('gulp-nodemon');

gulp.task('express', () => {
  nodemon({
    script: 'server/index.js',
    ignore: ['app']
  });
});
```

In this task, we are informing nodemon to ignore the changes under the `app` directory. The reason for this is that the `app` path is already watched by BrowserSync.

Now that we have the server, and the assets are served and reloaded automatically, we can merge these two tasks in order to run the project in development mode:

```
var httpProxy = require('http-proxy');

gulp.task('serve', ['browserify', 'express'], () => {
  var serverProxy = httpProxy.createProxyServer();

  browserSync({
    port: 9000,
    ui: {
      port: 9001
    },
    server: {
      baseDir: ['.tmp', 'app'],
      middleware: [
```

```
          function (req, res, next) {
            if (req.url.match(/^\/(api|avatar)\/.*/)) {
              serverProxy.web(req, res, {
                target: 'http://localhost:8000'
              });
            } else {
              next();
            }
          }
        ]
      }
    });

    gulp.watch([
      'app/*.html',
      'app/**/*.css',
      '.tmp/**/*.js'
    ]).on('change', reload);
  });
```

A new dependency should be installed, **http-proxy**. This dependency allows us to redirect all the API requests to the Express server so that BrowserSync does not try to serve these requests:

```
$ npm install --save-dev http-proxy
```

This time, we add the express task dependency to the serve task. As we are now running two servers on different ports, assets on 9000 and API on 8000, we add a middleware in BrowserSync to redirect the traffic that starts with /api/ or /avatar/ to the server located at port 8000.

Now, when you run the serve task from your command line, you will get an amazing development environment. Every time a file in the frontend is changed, the browser will be reloaded automatically with a new bundle. If a change in the server files is detected, the Express server will also be reloaded.

That's a great improvement for your development workflow; you will be more productive and forget about manual reloads.

Creating a production workflow

The development workflow that we built in the previous sections is an amazing improvement for the project; however, we are not finished yet. In this section, you will see how to optimize the project that is to be run in the production environments.

In this section, you will learn how to minimize your JavaScript and CSS files to obfuscate your source code and reduce the time the browser takes to load the asset files. The images can also be minified in order to reduce its weight without altering its appearance.

Gulp useref

The `gulp-useref` plugin processes your HTML files to concatenate your JavaScript and CSS assets into a single file. Please note that the JavaScript is already processed by Browserify, therefore, it is not necessary to process the JavaScript files with useref; on the other hand, CSS can be processed here.

You will need to install the plugin with npm as a development dependency:

```
$ npm install --save-dev gulp-useref
```

Then, to use it, you will need to create a new task. Let's call it `html`:

```
// ...

gulp.task('html', function() {
  var assets = $.useref.assets();

  return gulp.src('app/*.html')
    .pipe(assets)
    .pipe(assets.restore())
    .pipe($.useref())
    .pipe(gulp.dest('dist'));
});
```

The `gulp.src('app/*.html')` function grabs all the files with the `.html` extension. In our case, only the `index.html` file exists, therefore, it is the only file that will be processed. The `useref.assets()` function concatenates all the assets that are found in the HTML files and puts them in a stream, the `assets.restore()` function will restore the original stream of HTML files that are picked in the beginning.

When you call the `useref()` function, the HTML file is parsed in order to replace the assets files in a single HTML tag. For example, if you have five CSS files, it replaces these five link tags in the HTML file in a single tag that points to the concatenated version.

You should indicate the `useref` task how to concatenate the files with special tags in the HTML files:

```
<html>
<head>
<!-- ... -->
<!-- build:css(app) css/vendor.css -->
<link rel="stylesheet" href="css/bootstrap.css">
<link rel="stylesheet" href="css/main.css">
<!-- endbuild -->
<!-- ... -->
</head>
<!-- ... -->
</html>
```

You need add two HTML comments to the code, these comments have a special meaning for useref. Its syntax is as follows:

```
<!-- build:<type>(alternate search path) <path> -->
... HTML Markup, list of script / link tags.
<!-- endbuild -->
```

As we are processing CSS files, we use `css` as type, and the search path indicates where useref will look for the files. If we left this optional parameter blank, then it will use the root project path. The last `path` argument indicates where the concatenated CSS files will be put.

If you run the Gulp `html` task, you will get a concatenated file with all your styles under the `dist/css/vendor.css` path. The output HTML file will point to this file instead of the development ones:

```
<html>
<head>
<!-- ... -->
<link rel="stylesheet" href="css/vendor.css">
<!-- ... -->
</head>
<!-- ... -->
</html>
```

You can optimize the output CSS files by minifying them with the `gulp-minify-css` plugin. As you may have guessed, you should install the plugin with npm:

```
$ npm install --save-dev gulp-minify-css
```

Then you can use the plugin in your build process, as follows:

```
// ...
var minifyCss = require('gulp-minify-css');

gulp.task('html', function() {
  var assets = $.useref.assets();

  return gulp.src('app/*.html')
    .pipe(assets)
    .pipe(minifyCss())
    .pipe(assets.restore())
    .pipe($.useref())
    .pipe(gulp.dest('dist'));
});
```

This will minify the concatenated CSS file. However, as `useref` can process CSS and JavaScript files, the code can be buggy if a JavaScript build tag is added. To prevent errors, you can use the `gulp-if` plugin:

```
$ npm install --save-dev gulp-if gulp-uglify
```

This will also install `uglify` in order to also process the JavaScript files:

```
// ...

gulp.task('html', function() {
  var assets = $.useref.assets();

  return gulp.src('app/*.html')
    .pipe(assets)
    .pipe($.if('*.js', uglify()))
    .pipe($.if('*.css', minifyCss()))
    .pipe(assets.restore())
    .pipe($.useref())
    .pipe(gulp.dest('dist'));
});
```

With `gulp-if` we test if the file in the stream is a CSS or a JavaScript file and then apply the right transformation.

Image Optimization

When you are developing your project in the local machine, the assets load pretty fast as images and code live in the same computer; however, when you go to the production images, they travel through the Internet to your user machine.

With image optimization, we can compress these images in order to reduce the amount of data that your app downloads from the server. With node, you can use the `imagemin` package; however, as we are using Gulp, `gulp-imagemin` will do the job.

As we did earlier, you will need to install the plugin first:

```
$ npm install --save-dev gulp-imagemin
```

Now that the plugin is installed, we can use it:

```
gulp.task('images', function() {
  gulp.src('app/images/*.{jpg,gif,svg,png}')
    .pipe($.imagemin())
    .pipe(gulp.dest('dist/images'));
});
```

It grabs the images from the `app/images` path and applies the `imagemin()` process to each image.

Fonts

Fonts for Bootstrap are located under the `node_modules/` directory. If you install other type of fonts, such as Font Awesome, or download a specific fonts; they should be copied to the `dist/` directory. You can create a `fonts` task to do this, as shown in the following:

```
// ...

gulp.task('fonts', function () {
  return gulp.src([
    'app/{,styles/}fonts/**/*',
    'node_modules/bootstrap/dist/fonts/**/*'
  ])
    .pipe($.flatten())
    .pipe(gulp.dest('dist/fonts'));
});
```

Note that you will need to install the `gulp-flatten` plugin; this plugin will remove any prefix directory:

```
$ npm install --save-dev gulp-flatten
```

Bundle JavaScript files for production

The `browserify` task that we have is useful for development, it creates sourcemaps and the output is not minified. If you want to go to the production, you will need to remove the sourcemaps and minimize the output too.

For production environment, we will transform the ECMAScript 6 code into JavaScript in order to add support for these browsers that does not support for ECMAScript 6. Babel is the best transpiler at the moment to make this transformation.

The babelify plugin of Browserify will apply the transformations, as follows:

$ npm install --save-dev babelify

You will need to configure Babel before using the babelify plugin. In Babel 6, you have to install individual packages for the functions that you want to support. For this project, we support ES2015:

$ npm install --save-dev babel-preset-es2015

In the `.babelrc` file, you should configure the preset:

```
// .babelrc
{
  "presets": ["es2015"]
}
```

Once you have configured Babel properly, we can create the `browserify` task for production:

```
// Bundle files with browserify for production
gulp.task('browserify:dist', function () {
  // set up the browserify instance on a task basis
  var bundler = browserify({
    entries: 'app/js/main.js',
    // defining transforms here will avoid crashing your stream
    transform: [babelify, jstify]
  });

  return bundler.bundle()
    .on('error', $.util.log)
    .pipe(source('app.js'))
```

```
      .pipe(buffer())
      .pipe($.uglify())
      .pipe(gulp.dest('dist/js'));
});
```

This task does not generate sourcemaps and optimize the output.

Putting it all together

You have learned how to optimize several kind of assets: CSS, JavaScript, and images. Now let's put all this together in order to build our application. The `serve:dist` task wires all the processes into a pipeline:

```
gulp.task('serve:dist', ['browserify:dist', 'images', 'fonts',
'express'], () => {
  var serverProxy = httpProxy.createProxyServer();

  browserSync({
    port: 9000,
    ui: {
      port: 9001
    },
    server: {
      baseDir: 'dist',
      middleware: [
        function (req, res, next) {
          if (req.url.match(/^\/(api|avatar)\/.*/)) {
            serverProxy.web(req, res, {
              target: 'http://localhost:8000'
            });
          } else {
            next();
          }
        }
      ]
    }
  });
});
```

To test our pipeline, we can run the `serve:dist` task in the terminal:

```
$ gulp serve:dist
[11:18:04] Using gulpfile ~/Projects/mastering-backbone/ch07/gulpfile.js
[11:18:04] Starting 'browserify:dist'...
```

```
[11:18:04] Starting 'images'...

[11:18:04] Finished 'images' after 305 ms

[11:18:04] Starting 'fonts'...

[11:18:04] Starting 'express'...

[11:18:05] Finished 'express' after 141 ms

[11:18:05] gulp-imagemin: Minified 0 images

[11:18:05] [nodemon] 1.8.1

[11:18:05] [nodemon] to restart at any time, enter `rs`

[11:18:05] [nodemon] watching: *.*

[11:18:05] [nodemon] starting `node server/index.js`

Express server is running on port 8000

[11:18:08] Finished 'fonts' after 4.04 s

[11:18:12] Finished 'browserify:dist' after 8.02 s

[11:18:12] Starting 'serve:dist'...

[11:18:12] Finished 'serve:dist' after 40 ms

[11:18:12] [nodemon] restarting due to changes...

[BS] Access URLs:

 ------------------------------------

        Local: http://localhost:9000

     External: http://192.168.100.4:9000

 ------------------------------------

           UI: http://localhost:9001

  UI External: http://192.168.100.4:9001

 ------------------------------------

[BS] Serving files from: dist

[11:18:12] [nodemon] starting `node server/index.js`

Express server is running on port 8000
```

Notice how the tasks are executed by Gulp. After all these processes, the browser will automatically open while pointing to the `http://localhost:9000` address, running the application in the production environment.

Summary

In this chapter, we have seen how to use tools to build our Backbone application. First, you learned what a task runner is and the most popular choices available for Node. Then, we saw how Gulp works and creates tasks.

With Gulp, you can build a development environment and configure it in order to apply optimizations to your assets for the production environments. Gulp is stream-based, which means that you can grab a bunch of files from a `glob` specification and stream these files in order to apply transformations, such as compiling, concatenating, transpiling, and so on, as you need.

Task runners are amazing tools that allow you to automatize tasks. You can not only create development and production workflows, but also tasks for almost anything, which you don't want to repeat. For example, a task to make deployments.

In the next chapter, we will see how to test the Backbone applications. You will learn how to isolate and fake dependencies for easy testing, the what and how to make Backbone testing.

8
Testing Backbone Applications

It does not matter if you are an experienced programmer, it's very normal that you will commit mistakes in your code at some point in time. Nobody is perfect and errors happen all the time in software development. Your work as a developer is to minimize the number of defects that are in your software.

Errors can occur from different sources; an unexpected input, an error that is not handled properly, a change in a third-party plugin, a memory issue, and so on. Your code should be prepared to deal with these kind of things.

In the software industry, the rule of thumb is to always test your code. When you test your applications, the final product has a better quality as many defects have been detected and corrected before the users notice it.

Tests are not just undertaken to prevent bugs in the software. The following is a list of benefits that you get when you do the testing:

- Improves end-product quality
- Makes you confident with your application
- Allows you to refactor pieces of code safely
- Preserves functionality
- Simulates errors and improves your error handling code
- Improves your code, forcing you to make testable code

If you have never tested your software, now you have good reasons to start doing it. Make testing can slow down your development process at the start; however, you will see the benefits in the mid time.

In this chapter, you will learn the following:

- Which tools are available to test frontend applications
- What and how to test Backbone applications
- How to apply best practices for application testing
- How to run your tests automatically

Testing tools

A testing tool can be a library or framework that helps you to write tests for your applications and evaluate the results. Under testing tools, you can find the following:

- **Testing libraries**: This gives you a hook and functions to describe tests
- **Assertion libraries**: This gives you functions to make expectations
- **Test runners**: This discovers and runs your tests
- **Test coverage**: This tells you which parts of your code are tested and which are not
- **Test reports**: This makes reports in different formats such as HTML and JSON
- **Mocking, stubbing, faking tools**: These give you ways to make fake objects with predictable behavior
- **Module mocking**: This replaces a required module with a fake module and is useful to isolate modules
- **Stress tools**: This makes many requests to the applications in order to see how it behaves in high demand circumstances
- **Browser testing**: This emulates a user making inputs in the application as a whole

Explaining and showing how all these tools work is out of scope of this book. In this chapter, you will work with testing libraries, asserting libraries, testing runners, and mocking.

For JavaScript, there are many testing libraries available for you; however, two of them are more popular at the moment of writing this book: Jasmine and Mocha.

Mocha is a small library that allows you to write tests harness, it does not have any assertion functions by itself. What it means is that you should integrate Mocha with an assertion library of your choice; a very popular choice is to use a combination of Mocha and Chai.js.

Jasmine is more like a framework, it provides an API that is very similar to Mocha; however, it includes assertion functions. Therefore, it is simpler to use as you do not need to create an extra step.

For this book, we will use Jasmine as it is the most popular testing tool and is easier to start working with. In the same way as Mocha, you can use Jasmine as a test runner and select different types of reports.

Getting started with Jasmine

To write tests, you should create two things: test suites and specs. A spec (short for specification) is a piece of functionality that you are testing from your code; for example, if your code is calculating tax of 5% for $100.00, you would expect it to be $5. A test suite is a set of expectations that are grouped under a topic. In the preceding example, the test suite can be "Invoice totals calculation".

To start working with Jasmine, you should install it from npm, as follows:

```
$ npm install --save-dev jasmine
```

Then, you can start writing your tests. With Jasmine, you have two functions: describe() to create test suites and it() to make specs:

```
// specs/mathSpec.js
describe('Basic mathematicfunctions', () => {
it('should result 4 the sum of 2 + 2', () => {
  });

it('should result 1 the substract of 3 - 2', () => {
  });

it('should result 3 the division of 9 / 3', () => {
  });

it('should throw an error when divide by zero', () => {
  });
});
```

The preceding code defines a test suite for a hypothetical set of math functions. Notice how in the describe() function, you should write a text that tells the people what is the context of the tests; while in the it() function, the text should tells what are you testing.

Now, let's build the `math` functions for the test suite, as follows:

```
// app/js/math.js
var math = {
sum(a, b) {
return a + b;
  },

substract(a, b) {
return a - b;
  },

divide(a, b) {
if (b === 0) {
throw new Error('Can not divide by zero');
  }

return a / b;
  }
};

module.exports = math;
```

The `math` object has the necessary functions to pass the test suite; however, to actually test the `math` object, you will need to make a set of expectations.

Expectations

Expectations are functions that compare the output of a function with an expected output. In the following example, we call the `sum()` function with an input of 2 and 2. We are expecting that the result should be 4:

```
expect(sum(2, 2)).toEqual(4);
```

The `toEqual()` expectation function compares whether the output of the function and the expected value are equal; if both are the same, the test will pass, otherwise, it will fail. The following table shows the most common expectations in Jasmine, consult the documentation for a complete set of available expectation functions:

Expectation function	Description	Example
toEqual	The values should be exactly equal	expect('hello') .toEqual('hello')

Expectation function	Description	Example
`toMatch`	The value will be RegEx matched	`expect('Hello')` `    .toMatch(/[Hh]ello/)`

`toBeTruthy`	The value should be a truth value	`expect(true)`
		`    .toBeTruthy();`
		`expect(100)`
		`    .toBeTruthy();`

`toBeFalsy`	The value should be a false value	`expect(false)`
		`    .toBeFalsy();`
		`expect(null)`
		`    .toBeFalsy();`

`toThrowError`	This verifies that the function that is called throws an error	`expect(function() {`
		`math.divide(1, 0);`
		`}).toThrowError();`

After adding all the expectations to the example test suite that we have, the code should be something as follows:

```
// spec/mathSpec.js
var math = require('../app/js/math');

describe('Basic mathematic functions', () => {
it('should result 4 the sum of 2 + 2', () => {
expect(math.sum(2, 2)).toBe(4);
  });

it('should result 1 the substract of 3 - 2', () => {
expect(math.substract(3, 2)).toBe(1);
  });

it('should result 3 the division of 9 / 3', () => {
expect(math.divide(9, 3)).toBe(3);
  });

it('should throw an error when divide by zero', () => {
expect(() =>math.divide(9, 0)).toThrowError();
  });
});
```

To run the test suite, you should first configure the Jasmine test runner. To do this, you should create a script:

```
// spec/run.js
var Jasmine = require('jasmine');
var jasmine = new Jasmine();

jasmine.loadConfig({
spec_dir: 'spec',
spec_files: [
    '**/*[sS]pec.js'
  ]
});

jasmine.execute();
```

Jasmine will look for tests under the `spec/`directory, it will look for all those files that end with `spec.js` or `Spec.js`. As our test file is named `mathSpec.js`, the Jasmine test runner will load and run it, as shown in the following:

```
$ node spec/run.js
Started
....


4 specs, 0 failures
Finished in 0.008 seconds
```

You can see what happens if the test fails; for example, you change the sum test to 5 instead of 4:

```
$ node spec/run.js
Started
F...


Failures:
1) Basic mathematic functions should result 4 the sum of 2 + 2
  Message:
    Expected 4 to be 5.
  Stack:
    Error: Expected 4 to be 5.
```

```
at Object.<anonymous>(/path/to/your/project/spec/mathSpec.js:5:28)
```

```
4 specs, 1 failure
Finished in 0.009 seconds
```

Now, if you make a mistake, Jasmine will tell you what's wrong. Notice how Jasmine will inform you about the error:

"Basic mathematic functions should result 4 the sum of 2 + 2"

Then, it tells you that it was expecting 5 and instead received 4. Please note that it is very important what messages you put in the `describe()` and `it()` functions as they will help you to quickly diagnose what's wrong.

Testing asynchronous code

When you need to test a code that is asynchronous like an Ajax call, you will need to make an extra step. When you write the `it()` function, you should pass a `done` argument and Jasmine will put a callback function there, which you should call when the test is done.

To illustrate this, let's simulate an asynchronous task that sum two numbers, as follows:

```
var math = {
  // ...

asyncSum(a, b, callback) {
    // Will respond after 1.5 seconds.
setTimeout(function() {
callback(a + b);
    }, 1500);
  },

  // ...
};
```

Following the JavaScript standard, the `syncSum()` function receives a third argument, which is the callback function that will be called when the sum is ready. In the following example, the callback function will be called after 1,500 milliseconds:

```
math.asyncSum(2, 2, result => {
  // After 1500ms result will be equal to 4
});
```

To make a test with this function, we should pass a `done` callback to the `it()` function:

```
it('sums two numbers asynchronously', done => {
math.asyncSum(2, 2, function(result) {
expect(result).toEqual(4);
done();
  });
});
```

Karma test runner

Karma is a popular test runner for JavaScript, it works with many other testing libraries and frameworks such as Jasmine and Mocha. The Node test runner that comes with Jasmine is fine; however, Karma adds superpowers to the equation.

With Karma, you can run your tests on real web browsers such as Google Chrome, Firefox, Opera, and so on. Once Karma is set and running, it will take care of lookup for the files to test, run it, and then give you a report.

You will need to install Karma before starting to work with it:

```
$ npm install --save-dev karma karma-jasmine karma-browserify karma-
chrome-launcher karma-spec-reporter
```

Then, you can configure Karma with a script named `karma.conf.js`:

```
// Karma configuration
// http://karma-runner.github.io/0.12/config/configuration-file.html

module.exports = function(config) {
  'use strict';

config.set({
    // enable / disable watching file and executing tests whenever
    // any file changes
autoWatch: true,

    // base path, that will be used to resolve files and exclude
basePath: '',

    // testing framework to use (jasmine/mocha/qunit/...)
frameworks: ['browserify', 'jasmine'],

    // list of files / patterns to load in the browser
files: [
```

```
        'spec/**/*Spec.js'
    ],

    // preprocess matching files before serving them to
    // the browser available preprocessors:
    // https://npmjs.org/browse/keyword/karma-preprocesso
preprocessors: {
        'spec/**/*Spec.js': ['browserify']
    },

    // Cobfigure how to bundle the test files with Browserify
browserify: {
debug: true,
transform: ['jstify'],
extensions: ['.js', '.tpl']
    },

    // report on console and growl if available
    //
    // More info about growl notifications on
    // http://mattn.github.io/growl-for-linux/
    // http://growl.info/
reporters: ['spec'],

    // list of files / patterns to exclude
exclude: [],

    // web server port
port: 9876,

    // enable / disable colors in the output (reporters and logs)
colors: true,

    // level of logging
    // possible values:
    // LOG_DISABLE || LOG_ERROR || LOG_WARN ||
    // LOG_INFO || LOG_DEBUG
logLevel: config.LOG_INFO,

    // Continuous Integration mode
    // if true, it capture browsers, run tests and exit
singleRun: false,

    // Start these browsers, currently available:
```

```
        // - Chrome
        // - ChromeCanary
        // - Firefox
        // - Opera
        // - Safari (only Mac)
        // - PhantomJS
        // - IE (only Windows)
    browsers: ['Chrome']
    });
    };
```

The `files` field tells to Karma which files will be tested in the `glob` format. The `preprocessors` field tells to Karma whether the files selected from the `files` field should be preprocessed before running the tests. As we are using Browserify to manage the dependencies, we should preprocess the files with Browserify in order to create a test bundle.

You can choose how you want Karma to report the test status to you. The `reporters` field makes this possible, you can search for more reporters available; however, the `spec` reporter is one of the most used.

Once Karma is configured, you can run the tests that we have with Karma instead of the Jasmine test runner:

```
$ ./node_modules/karma/bin/karma start
```

You can automatize how you run Karma with Gulp, after all that's its job:

```
// configuration of Gulp
```

What and how to test Backbone applications

Backbone library has different components, each one with its own intentions and responsibilities, that's why you have to test them differently. Keep it in mind that you should only test your code and not the Backbone built-in functionalities.

In the next sections, you will see what are the parts of your Backbone applications and how to test them; we will start from simple things and then go for more complex ones. Then, you will learn how to isolate modules to only test one module at time.

Testing models and collections

The most basic test is to ensure that models and collections have the right properties set in order to prevent accidental changes in its properties. In the case of models, you can test the default values when a new contact is created and verify that the `url` attribute is right:

```
// spec/apps/contacts/models/contactSpec.js
var Contact = require('../../../../app/js/apps/contacts/models/
contact');

describe('Contact model', () => {
describe('creating a new contact', () => {
it('has the default values', () => {
var contact = new Contact();

expect(contact.get('name')).toEqual('');
expect(contact.get('phone')).toEqual('');
expect(contact.get('email')).toEqual('');
expect(contact.get('address1')).toEqual('');
expect(contact.get('address2')).toEqual('');
expect(contact.get('avatar')).toEqual(null);
    });
  });

it('has the rigthurl', () => {
var contact = new Contact();
expect(contact.url()).toEqual('/api/contacts');
  });
});
```

For collections, you can verify that the `url` is right:

```
// spec/apps/contacts/collections/contactCollectionSpec.js
varContactCollection = require('../../../../app/js/apps/contacts/
collections/contactCollection');

describe('Contac collection', () => {
it('has the rigthurlRoot', () => {
var collection = new ContactCollection();
expect(collection.url).toEqual('/api/contacts');
  });
});
```

Testing views

Views manage the relationship between data (such as, models or collections) and the user interactions (DOM). In the case of views, you should test for the following:

- Rendering: Given a model or collection, you should verify that the output HTML is the right one
- Events: This verifies that the DOM events are handled correctly
- Model changes: If the model changes something, the view should be in sync

For this example, we are going to test the ContactForm view; the responsibility of this view is to show a form to the user and then get the user input to update a model.

When making test on views, it is recommended to use a fake model and not the original Contact model. The main reason for this is to isolate the ContactView object so that if a test fails, you will know that the error is isolated in the view and does not depend on the Contact model.

You can start testing whether the rendered HTML is right, as follows:

```
var Backbone = require('backbone');
var ContactForm = require('../../../../app/js/apps/contacts/views/
contactForm');

describe('Contact form', () => {
var fakeContact;

beforeEach(() => {
fakeContact = new Backbone.Model({
name: 'John Doe',
facebook: 'https://www.facebook.com/john.doe',
twitter: '@john.doe',
github: 'https://github.com/johndoe',
google: 'https://plus.google.com/johndoe'
    });
  });

it('has the rigth class', () => {
var view = new ContactForm({model: fakeContact});
expect(view.className).toEqual('form-horizontal');
  });

it('renders the rigth HTML', () => {
```

```
var view = new ContactForm({model: fakeContact});

view.render();

expect(view.$el.html()).toContain(fakeContact.get('name'));
expect(view.$el.html()).toContain(fakeContact.get('twitter'));
expect(view.$el.html()).toContain(fakeContact.get('github'));
expect(view.$el.html()).toContain(fakeContact.get('google'));
expect(view.$el.html())
.toContain(fakeContact.get('facebook'));
  });
});
```

Note how in the test, we are looking in the output HTML if contains a specific text on it. You can use specific selectors instead:

```
expect(view.$el.find('#name').val())
.toContain(fakeContact.get('name'));
```

However, it is not recommended to do this in unstable applications as the design can quickly change and the tests will fail even if the name is on the screen:

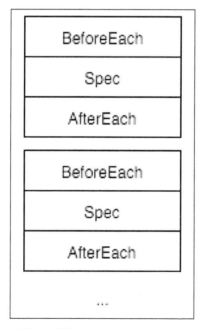

Figure 8.1 Jasmine testing functions

Figure 8.1 illustrates the relationship between the `beforeEach()`, `afterEach()`, and `it()` functions. When you define one or more `beforeEach()` functions in `describe()`, then all the `beforeEach()` functions will always be executed before the `it()` functions. This feature is very useful as you can ensure the same initial conditions for each test.

In the example test suite for the `ContactForm` object, we are ensuring that `fakeContact` always has the same attributes; if you change something in the model under an `it()` function, the next function will always get a clean `fakeContact` model to test.

The `ContactForm` object has a **Save** button that triggers a `form:save` event when it is clicked; to test this, you can listen for the event on a Jasmine **spy function**. A spy function is a function that does nothing but record when and how it is called. Then, you can use it to make expectation in it:

```
it('triggers a form:save event when save button is cliecked', () => {
var view = new ContactForm({model: fakeContact});
var callback = jasmine.createSpy('callback');

view.on('form:save', callback);
view.render();

// Emulate a user click
view.$el.find('#save').trigger('click');

expect(callback).toHaveBeenCalled();
});
```

The `createSpy()` method of Jasmine creates a spy function that will be used as the event handler for the `from:save` event. Then, it emulates a click event on the save button and tests whether the `callback` function was called.

We can go a step forward and check whether the function is called with the model as argument:

```
expect(callback).toHaveBeenCalledWith(mockContact);
```

Now is time to test when the user makes the input in the form and then click the **Save** button; what we are expecting from it is that the model changes with the input values:

```
it('updates the model when the save button is clicked', () => {
var view = new ContactForm({model: fakeContact});
var callback = jasmine.createSpy('callback');
varexpectedValues = {
```

```
    name: 'Jane Doe',
    facebook: 'https://www.facebook.com/example',
    twitter: '@example',
    github: 'https://github.com/example',
    google: 'https://plus.google.com/example'
      };

    view.on('form:save', callback);
    view.render();

      // Change the input fields
      view.$el.find('#name').val(expectedValues.name);
    view.$el.find('#facebook').val(expectedValues.facebook);
    view.$el.find('#twitter').val(expectedValues.twitter);
    view.$el.find('#github').val(expectedValues.github);
    view.$el.find('#google').val(expectedValues.google);

      // Emulate a change events on all input fields
    view.$el.find('input').trigger('change');

      // Emulate a user click
    view.$el.find('#save').trigger('click');

    // Get the argument passed to the callback function
    var callArgs = callback.calls.argsFor(0);
    var model = callArgs[0];

    expect(model.get('name')).toEqual(expectedValues.name);
    expect(model.get('facebook')).toEqual(expectedValues.facebook);
    expect(model.get('twitter')).toEqual(expectedValues.twitter);
    expect(model.get('github')).toEqual(expectedValues.github);
    expect(model.get('google')).toEqual(expectedValues.google);
    });
```

In this test, we are changing the values in the input fields and then clicking the save button in the form. The `callback` spy function records how the `form:save` event is triggered and extracts the argument passed to it. We can use this argument to test whether the model was updated as expected.

Testing controllers

Controllers are more complex than test as they have more dependencies than the models, collections, and views. If you explore the code on these objects, you will see that the only dependencies that they have are Backbone and Underscore.

You can test the controllers with all its dependencies, which means that while testing the `ContactEditor` controller, you will be testing all the views and models attached to it as the module requires these objects.

That's not good for unit testing as you will end up with integration tests instead. If the `Contact` model has a defect, then `ContactEditor` will fail, even if it does not have any error in it.

You need to isolate the modules from the mess of other modules. Keep in mind that you should trust your libraries as they will already have their test suites. We need a mechanism to fake the dependencies of a module.

With dependency injection, you can overwrite the `require()` function, instead of loading the script that points, in order to use a fake object. This will guarantee that the code that is being tested is isolated and its behavior is predictable for unit testing.

Mocking dependencies

There are two main choices to mock dependencies in Node: `rewire` and `proxyquireify`; with these libraries, you can overwrite the original dependencies of a module in order to use a fake version instead.

With Browserify, you should have `proxyquireify`. Install it with npm, as follows:

```
$ npm install --save-dev proxyquirefy
```

Once the library is installed, we need to add a proper configuration in the Karma configuration file:

```
// ...

browserify: {
debug: true,
plugin: ['proxyquireify/plugin'],
transform: ['jstify'],
extensions: ['.js', '.tpl']
},

// ...
```

You should initialize `proxyquireify` before using it. As `proxyquireify` overwrites the original `require()` function, it should be initialized before being used. The initialization function returns a function object that is similar to the original `require()` function; however, with the the extra functionality of fake dependencies, as shown in the following:

```
var proxyquire = require('proxyquireify')(require);
```

The `proxyquire` object can be used to load modules:

```
var ContactViewer = proxyquire('./contacts/contactViewer');
```

When you load a module with `proxyquireify`, you can use a second argument to overwrite the original dependencies. It is an object where the keys are the name of the dependencies and the values are the object that will substitute the original dependency:

```
var targetFile = '../../app/js/apps/contacts/contactViewer';
var fakes = {
'./views/ContactView': Backbone.View
}
var ContactViewer = proxyquire(targetFile, fakes);
```

This configuration will replace the `ContactView` object with an empty `Backbone. View` object so that when testing the `ContactViewer` object, the module will not load the original `ContactView` module.

Fake objects

A fake object is a simple object that has the same functions as an original one; however, with a predictable behavior so that you can use fake objects to isolate the module under test. For example, all our controllers depend on the `App` object to work; however, it is not a good idea to use the real `App` object for the purpose of testing. If the `App` object has an error, then the controller test will fail.

A fake for the `App` object is as shown in the following:

```
// spec/fakes/app.js
'use strict';

var fakeRouter = {
navigate: jasmine.createSpy()
};

var FakeApp = {
```

```
router:   fakeRouter,

notifySuccess(message) {
this.lastSuccessMessage= message;
   },

notifyError(message) {
this.lastErrorMessage = message;
   },

reset() {
deletethis.lastSuccessMessage;
deletethis.lastErrorMessage;
this.router.navigate = jasmine.createSpy();
  }
};

_.extend(FakeApp, Backbone.Events);

module.exports = FakeApp;
```

This simple object can simulate to be the real App object, as you can see the object does nothing; however, it will be useful in the next section for testing the ContactEditor controller.

Regions can also be faked in order to remove all the overheads of the original region:

```
// spec/fakes/region.js
'use strict';

class FakeRegion {
show(view) {
view.render();
  }
}

module.exports = FakeRegion;
```

It is very simple, just to render the view that is passed to it.

Testing ContactEditor

The `ContactEditor` controller's responsibility is to render the necessary views in order to allow the user to update or create new contacts. It is closely related to many views and the `Contact` model.

We are going to use `proxyquireify` to isolate the `ContactEditor` controller and instead of using the real objects, we will fake most of them. The first test is to check whether the subapplication is rendered in the right region:

```
// spec/apps/contacts/contactEditor.js
var proxyquery = require('proxyquireify')(require);
var Backbone = require('backbone');

var FakeRegion = require('../../fakes/region');
var fakes = {
'./views/contactPreview': Backbone.View,
'./views/phoneListView': Backbone.View,
'./views/emailListView': Backbone.View,
'./collections/phoneCollection': Backbone.Collection,
'./collections/emailCollection': Backbone.Collection
};

var ContactEditor = proxyquery('../../../app/js/apps/contacts/
contactEditor', fakes);

describe('Contact editor', () => {
var fakeContact;
var editor;
var region;

beforeEach(() => {
region = new FakeRegion();
editor = new ContactEditor({region});
fakeContact = new Backbone.Model({
name: 'John Doe',
facebook: 'https://www.facebook.com/john.doe',
twitter: '@john.doe',
github: 'https://github.com/johndoe',
google: 'https://plus.google.com/johndoe'
});
});

describe('showing a contact editor', () => {
it('renders the editor in the given region', () => {
```

```
spyOn(region, 'show').and.callThrough();
editor.showEditor(fakeContact);
expect(region.show).toHaveBeenCalled();
    });
  });
});
```

We are faking almost all the views of the `ContactEditor` controller, we don't need the real views as we are not testing the output HTML, that's a job for view testing. The only view that is not faked is the `FormLayout` view:

```javascript
// spec/fakes/formLayout.js
'use strict';

var Common = require('../../app/js/common');

class FakeFormLayout extends Common.Layout {
constructor(options) {
super(options);
this.template = '<div class="phone-list-container" />' +
                    '<div class="email-list-container" />';

this.regions = {
phones: '.phone-list-container',
emails: '.email-list-container'
    };
  }
}

module.exports = FakeFormLayout;
```

Then add the fake, as follows:

```javascript
var FakeFormLayout = require('../../fakes/formLayout');

var fakes = {
'./views/contactPreview': Backbone.View,
'./views/phoneListView': Backbone.View,
'./views/emailListView': Backbone.View,
'./views/contactForm': FakeFormLayout,
'./collections/phoneCollection': Backbone.Collection,
'./collections/emailCollection': Backbone.Collection
};

// ...
```

In the `ContactEditor` controller, we are listening for `avatar:selected` of the `ContactPreview` view, we should ensure that the event is handled correctly. However, we have a problem, we cannot access the view instance. To make the controller testable, it is a common practice to put the views as attributes of the controller, as shown in the following code:

```
class ContactEditor {
  // ...

showEditor(contact) {
    // Data
var phonesData = contact.get('phones') || [];
var emailsData = contact.get('emails') || [];
this.phones = new PhoneCollection(phonesData);
this.emails = new EmailCollection(emailsData);

    // Create the views
this.layout = new ContactFormLayout({model: contact});
this.phonesView = new PhoneListView({
collection: this.phones
});
this.emailsView = new EmailListView({
collection: this.emails
});
this.contactForm = new ContactForm({model: contact});
this.contactPreview = new ContactPreview({
controller: this,
model: contact
    });

    // Render the views
this.region.show(this.layout);
this.layout.getRegion('form').show(this.contactForm);
this.layout.getRegion('preview').show(this.contactPreview);
this.contactForm.getRegion('phones').show(this.phonesView);
this.contactForm.getRegion('emails').show(this.emailsView);

this.listenTo(this.contactForm, 'form:save',
this.saveContact);
this.listenTo(this.contactForm, 'form:cancel', this.cancel);
this.listenTo(this.contactForm, 'phone:add', this.addPhone);
this.listenTo(this.contactForm, 'email:add', this.addEmail);

this.listenTo(this.phonesView, 'item:phone:deleted',
```

```
(view, phone) => {
this.deletePhone(phone);
    });
this.listenTo(this.emailsView, 'item:email:deleted',
  (view, email) => {
this.deleteEmail(email);
    });

    // When avatar is selected, we can save it inmediatly if the
    // contact already exists on the server, otherwise just
    // remember the file selected
this.listenTo(this.contactPreview, 'avatar:selected',
blob => {
this.avatarSelected = blob;

if (!contact.isNew()) {
this.uploadAvatar(contact);
      }
    });
  }

  // ...
}
```

With this change, we can make the proper test, it verifies that the `avatarSelected` property is set when the `contactPreview` view selects an image:

```
it('binds the avatar:selected event in the contact preview', () => {
var expectedBlob = new Blob(['just text'], {
type: 'text/plain'
});

editor.showEditor(fakeContact);
// Fake the uploadAvatar method to prevent side effects
editor.uploadAvatar = jasmine.createSpy();

editor.contactPreview.trigger('avatar:selected', expectedBlob);
expect(editor.avatarSelected).toEqual(expectedBlob);
});
```

The core functionality of the `ContactEditor` controller is to save the contact properly when the user clicks on the **Save** button, as follows:

```
describe('Contact editor', () => {
  // ...
describe('saving a contact', () => {
beforeEach(() => {
jasmine.Ajax.install();

    // Fake the contact url, it is not important here
    fakeContact.url = '/fake/contact';

    // Fake upload avatar, we are not testing this feature
editor.uploadAvatar = function(contact, options) {
options.success();
    };

editor.showEditor(fakeContact);
  });

afterEach(() => {
jasmine.Ajax.uninstall();
FakeApp.reset();
  });
  }
}
```

In this test case, the controller will call the `save()` method in the model to save the contact and Backbone will make an Ajax call to the server. When you are testing, you should not make real server connections as that will make your tests slow and prone to failing.

With the `jasmine-ajax` plugin, you can fake the Ajax calls so that you will have a total control of how the test behaves. You will need to install the package first:

`$ npm install --save-devkarma-jasmine-ajax`

Then, update the configuration of Karma to include the plugin, as follows:

```
frameworks: ['browserify', 'jasmine-ajax', 'jasmine'],
```

The plugin overwrites the original `XMLHttpRequest` object, therefore, it's important to initialize the Ajax plugin before starting your test and restore the original object once your test is done.

In the `beforeEach()` function, we will initialize the plugin by calling `jasmine.Ajax.install()` and restore the original `XMLHttpRequest` object with `jasmine.Ajax.uninstall()` in `afterEach()`.

When your application makes an Ajax call, the plugin will catch the request and you can then inspect the request or fake the response, as follows:

```
it('shows a success message when the contact is saved', () => {
editor.saveContact(fakeContact);

jasmine.Ajax.requests.mostRecent().respondWith({
status: '200',
contentType: 'application/json',
responseText: '{}'
    });

expect(FakeApp.lastSuccessMessage).toEqual('Contact saved');
expect(FakeApp.router.navigate)
.toHaveBeenCalledWith('contacts', true);
});
```

In the preceding test, we saved the contact and faked an HTTP 200 response. When this happens, the application will show a success message and redirect the application to the contact list.

If the server responds with an error, then the application will show an error message and not make a redirection to the contact list:

```
it('shows an error message when the contact cant be saved', () => {
editor.saveContact(fakeContact);

jasmine.Ajax.requests.mostRecent().respondWith({
status: '400',
contentType: 'application/json',
responseText: '{}'
    });

expect(FakeApp.lastErrorMessage)
.toEqual('Something goes wrong');
expect(FakeApp.router.navigate)
.not.toHaveBeenCalled();
});
```

Another thing that the `saveContact()` method does is to set the `phones` and `emails` attributes in the contact model. The test will ensure that the attributes are sent to the server correctly, as shown in the following code:

```
it('saves the model with the phones and emails added', () => {
var expectedPhone = {
description: 'test',
phone: '555 5555'
  };
var expectedEmail = {
description: 'test',
phone: 'john.doe@example.com'
  };

editor.phones = new Backbone.Collection([expectedPhone]);
editor.emails = new Backbone.Collection([expectedEmail]);
editor.saveContact(fakeContact);

var requestText = jasmine.Ajax.requests.mostRecent().params;
var request = JSON.parse(requestText);

expect(request.phones.length).toEqual(1);
expect(request.emails.length).toEqual(1);
expect(request.phones).toContain(expectedPhone);
expect(request.emails).toContain(expectedEmail);
});
```

We are setting a list of `phones` and `emails` and then test whether the server receives the right request.

If the contact is not valid, then the controller will not send anything to the server:

```
it('does not save the contact if the model is not valid', () => {
  // Emulates an invalid model
fakeContact.isValid = function() {
return false;
  };

editor.saveContact(fakeContact);
expect(jasmine.Ajax.requests.count()).toEqual(0);
});
```

The ContactEditor object should upload the avatar image only if the model is new. If the model not is new, then the avatar is uploaded immediately when the user selects the image:

```
it('uploads the selected avatar if model is new', () => {
  // Emulates a new model
fakeContact.isNew= function() {
return true;
  };

  editor.uploadAvatar = jasmine.createSpy('uploadAvatar');
  editor.saveContact(fakeContact);

  jasmine.Ajax.requests.mostRecent().respondWith({
  status: '200',
  contentType: 'application/json',
  responseText: '{}'
  });

  expect(editor.uploadAvatar).toHaveBeenCalled();
});

it('does not upload the selected avatar if model is not new', () => {
  // Emulates a not new model
fakeContact.isNew= function() {
return false;
  };

  editor.uploadAvatar = jasmine.createSpy('uploadAvatar');
  editor.saveContact(fakeContact);

  jasmine.Ajax.requests.mostRecent().respondWith({
  status: '200',
  contentType: 'application/json',
  responseText: '{}'
  });

  expect(editor.uploadAvatar).not.toHaveBeenCalled();
});
```

Testing the subapplication Façade

The subapplication façade's responsibility is to create the model or collect objects and create the appropriate subapplication controller to render the fetched data. To show the contact editor, the Façade should fetch the contact by its ID and then run the `ContactEditor` subapplication:

```
var proxyquery = require('proxyquireify')(require);

var FakeApp = require('../../fakes/app');
var FakeRegion = require('../../fakes/region');
var FakeContactEditor = require('../../fakes/contactEditor');

var fakes = {
'../../app': FakeApp,
'./contactEditor': FakeContactEditor,
'./contactList': {},
'./contactViewer': {}
};

var ContactsApp = proxyquery('../../../app/js/apps/contacts/app',
fakes);

describe('Contacts application facade', () => {
var app;
var region;

function respond(request) {
var fakeResponse = {
name: 'John Doe',
facebook: 'https://www.facebook.com/john.doe',
twitter: '@john.doe',
github: 'https://github.com/johndoe',
google: 'https://plus.google.com/johndoe'
};

request.respondWith({
status: 200,
contentType: 'application/json',
responseText: JSON.stringify(fakeResponse)
});
}

beforeEach(() => {
```

```
    region = new FakeRegion();
    app = new ContactsApp({region});

    jasmine.Ajax.install();
      });

    afterEach(() => {
    jasmine.Ajax.uninstall();
      });

    describe('showing contact editor', () => {

      });
    });
```

The setup for this test suite is very similar to the controller. We should fake the `Ajax`
calls and create a Façade object that is to be used on the specs. Our first test will be to
verify that it is fetching the correct data:

```
    it('fetches data from the server', () => {
    app.showContactEditorById('1');

    var request = jasmine.Ajax.requests.mostRecent();
    expect(request.url).toEqual('/api/contacts/1');
    });
```

The Façade should trigger `loading: start` when fetching the data from the server:

```
    it('triggers a loading:start event', () => {
    var callback = jasmine.createSpy('callback');

    FakeApp.on('loading:start', callback);
    app.showContactEditorById('1');

    expect(callback).toHaveBeenCalled();
    });
```

Then, it should stop when the request is fulfilled:

```
    it('triggers a loading:stop event when the contact is loaded', () => {
    var callback = jasmine.createSpy('callback');

    FakeApp.on('loading:stop', callback);
    app.showContactEditorById('1');
    respond(jasmine.Ajax.requests.mostRecent());

    expect(callback).toHaveBeenCalled();
    });
```

Finally, it should show the editor:

```
it('shows the rigth contact', () => {
spyOn(FakeContactEditor.prototype, 'showEditor');
app.showContactEditorById('1');
respond(jasmine.Ajax.requests.mostRecent());

expect(FakeContactEditor.prototype.showEditor)
.toHaveBeenCalled();

var args = FakeContactEditor.prototype
.showEditor.calls.argsFor(0);
var model = args[0];

expect(model.get('id')).toEqual('1');
expect(model.get('name')).toEqual('John Doe');
});
```

Summary

If you want to build robust applications with minimum defects, you should test your code. Even if you are very good at coding, sometimes you may forget a validation or break a dependency and won't know about it until the final user of your application finds the bug.

As a professional developer, you should make sure that your code is always ready for production; one way to successfully do it is to run tests in your development workflow. Another benefit of testing applications is that you will gain confidence in your code, which means that you can improve your code without the fear of breaking something accidentally.

In Backbone, testing depends on the responsibility of the object that you are testing. Models, views, controllers, and facades are tested in their own way. However, it doesn't matter what the object is, Jasmine does a great work in order to help you to make a good test battery.

In the next chapter, you will learn how to deploy your Backbone application to a server for production and how to build a production environment for your applications. You will setup a Heroku instance if you don't want to mess with the server configuration internals or want to see how all the parts are connected in deep. I will show you how to configure an Ubuntu server in order to make your deployments.

Deploying to Production

9

You have built a great project: it is modularized, has tests, has been automatized to do common tasks, and finally you have built a production version with Gulp; however, now how do you deploy to a production server?

This chapter examines what to do with the production version of your project. Here, you will see how to run your node server and frontend assets in a production environment.

There are many choices to run your project in production mode; you can deploy on a bare metal server, use a virtual machine, on a shared host such as DigitalOcean or RackSpace, or maybe just deploy it to a **PaaS (Platform as a service)** service such as Heroku.

In the following section, we will see how to deploy to an Heroku instance, this is the easiest way to make a deployment as you don't have to worry about the server details and you can manage all the configurations in a single configuration file.

If you already have your own infrastructure or simply prefer to work with server instances such as DigitalOcean or RackSpace virtual server, we will show you how to configure a production environment on a server, where you have access to a shell.

Heroku

Heroku is a PaaS, which means that you don't have to worry about the details of the server configuration where you are deploying your code, you only focus on your code; Heroku will do the difficult job with the infrastructure configuration.

Instead of using a shell to install, configure, and tune up your packages in order to run in production mode, you only have to edit a configuration file and publish your changes with the standard `git push` command.

Dynos

Heroku uses lightweight Linux containers that run a single command in order to run your projects in the Heroku platform. Heroku calls these containers Dynos. A Dyno can host your code and run it as a single process in an isolated Linux environment.

If you don't have an experience in Linux containers such as Docker, you can imagine a container to be like a small virtual machine without hardware emulation; a Linux container uses the same kernel as the host machine, it means that you don't need to emulate hardware:

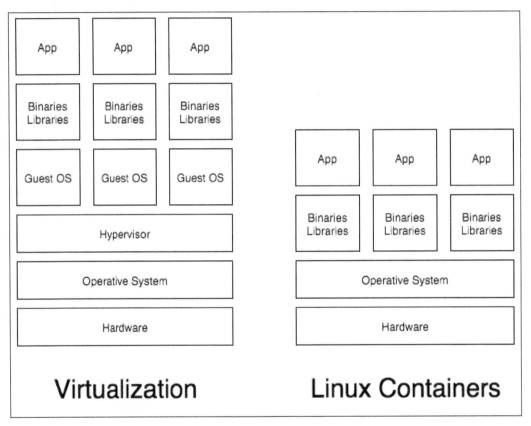

Figure 9.1 Difference between virtualization and containers

By default, Heroku will use Celadon Cedar stack to build Dynos; and Celadon Cedar stack is based on the Ubuntu distribution. With this is mind, you will get an Ubuntu-like distribution, where you can run your code written on:

- Ruby on Rails
- Node.js

- Java or Spring
- Python or Django
- Clojure
- Scala or Play
- PHP
- Go

Dyno comes in three different types, as shown in the following:

- **Web Dynos**: They are used to run the server code and respond to HTTP requests.
- **Worker Dynos**: They are useful for background jobs such as image processor.
- **One-off Dynos**: Their purpose is to provide maintenance to the other two Dyno types.

As you may have guessed that in this book, we will only use the Web Dynos with Node.js to run our `Contacts app`.

Getting started with Heroku

The first thing to do in order to start working with Heroku is to register with the service, as follows:

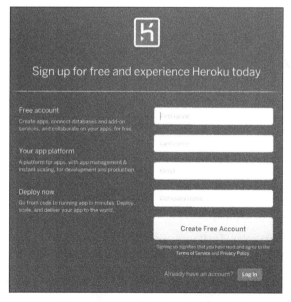

Figure 9.2 Heroku registration form

Once you are registered in the platform, you will need to install the Heroku Toolbelt in your host; there are versions available for Linux, Mac OS X, and Windows. After the installation process, you can use the `heroku` command to authenticate the service:

```
$heroku login
Enter your Heroku credentials.
Email: your.email@example.com
Password (typing will be hidden):
Authentication successful.
```

After you have authenticated with the Heroku service, you can start creating Dynos using the create command:

```
$ heroku create
Creating enigmatic-anchorage-3587... done, stack is cedar-14
https://enigmatic-anchorage-3587.herokuapp.com/ | https://git.heroku.com/
enigmatic-anchorage-3587.git
Git remote heroku added
```

When you create a new Dyno on Heroku, it generates a random name for your Dyno. In the preceding example, the name is `enigmatic-anchorage-3587` and you can access to your Dyno at `https://enigmatic-anchorage-3587.herokuapp.com`:

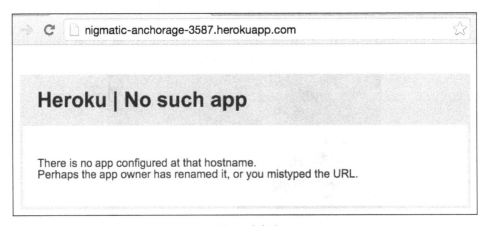

Figure 9.3 Dyno default output

You can deploy your application by pushing your changes to the Git server located at `https://git.heroku.com/enigmatic-anchorage-3587.git`. You will need to add this address as a remote server in your repo:

```
$ git remote add heroku https://git.heroku.com/enigmatic-anchorage-3587.
git
```

If you make a push right now, the deployment will not work and that's because you need to tell Heroku how to run your project; this is done with a configuration file named `Procfile` that you should put in the application root:

```
web: node server/index.js
```

The code is very simple, run the `server/index.js` script. You can test whether the configuration is working with the `local` command; this command is very useful in order to find bugs or issues before making a real deployment:

```
$ heroku local

Installing Heroku Toolbelt v4... done

Setting up iojs-v3.2.0... done

Installing core plugins heroku-apps, heroku-fork, heroku-git, heroku-local, heroku-run, heroku-status... done

Downloading forego-0.16.1 to /Users/abiee/.heroku... done

forego | starting web.1 on port 5000

web.1   | Server running
```

You can access the server using the browser at the http://localhost:8000/ URL. If you don't get any issues, you can make a real deployment by pushing the code at the master branch:

```
$ git checkout master

$ gulp build

$ git add .

$ git commit "Deployment build"

$ git push heroku master

Counting objects: 63, done.

Delta compression using up to 8 threads.

Compressing objects: 100% (57/57), done.

Writing objects: 100% (63/63), 380.85 KiB | 0 bytes/s, done.

Total 63 (delta 3), reused 0 (delta 0)

remote: Compressing source files... done.

remote: Building source:

remote:

remote: -----> Node.js app detected

remote:

remote: -----> Creating runtime environment

remote:

remote:           NPM_CONFIG_LOGLEVEL=error
```

```
remote:          NPM_CONFIG_PRODUCTION=true
remote:          NODE_ENV=production
remote:          NODE_MODULES_CACHE=true
remote:
remote: -----> Installing binaries
remote:          engines.node (package.json):  unspecified
remote:          engines.npm (package.json):   unspecified (use default)
remote:
remote:          Resolving node version (latest stable) via semver.io...
remote:          Downloading and installing node 0.12.7...
remote:          Using default npm version: 2.11.3
remote:
remote: -----> Restoring cache
remote:          Skipping cache (new runtime signature)
remote:
remote: -----> Building dependencies
remote:          Pruning any extraneous modules
remote:          Installing node modules (package.json)
...
remote: -----> Caching build
remote:          Clearing previous node cache
remote:          Saving 1 cacheDirectories (default):
remote:          - node_modules
remote:
remote: -----> Build succeeded!
remote:          ├── backbone@1.2.2
remote:          ├── body-parser@1.13.3
remote:          ├── browser-sync@2.8.2
remote:          ├── express@4.13.3
remote:          ├── http@0.0.0
remote:          ├── http-proxy@1.11.2
remote:          ├── jquery@2.1.4
remote:          ├── lodash@3.10.1
remote:          ├── morgan@1.6.1
remote:          ├── multer@1.0.3
remote:          └── underscore@1.8.3
```

```
remote:
remote: -----> Discovering process types
remote:        Procfile declares types -> web
remote:
remote: -----> Compressing... done, 25.4MB
remote: -----> Launching... done, v3
remote:        https://enigmatic-anchorage-3587.herokuapp.com/ deployed
to Heroku
remote:
remote: Verifying deploy.... done.
To https://git.heroku.com/enigmatic-anchorage-3587.git
```

In the output logs, you can see what Heroku is doing:

- Heroku detects what kind of project it is in order to know how to build the right environment. It could detect that it is a `Node` project due the presence of the `package.json` file.

- Knowing that it is a Node project, it could set some useful environment variables in order to run the project in production mode. You can use the `NODE_ENV` environment variable in your code in order to use some special configuration for production environments.

- Then, read the `package.json` file to see what version of node to install. You can specify a node version to install with the engines configuration, as follows:

```
"engines": {
  "node": "^0.12.21"
},
```

- After the right node version is installed in the Dyno, Heroku will install the project dependencies that are specified in the `package.json` file.

- Then, it will look up for the configuration for the kind of Dyno that is launched and see how to run the project at `Procfile`.

- Finally, it will compress the build and launch the project.

Once the project is running in the Heroku infrastructure, you can see the result at
`https://enigmatic-anchorage-3587.herokuapp.com/`:

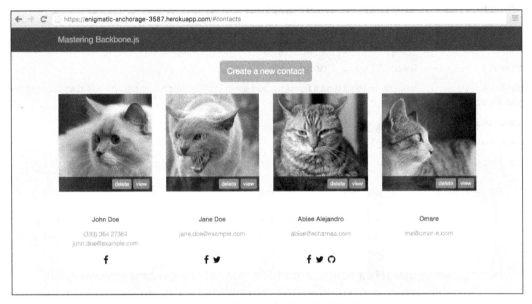

Figure 9.4 Application deployed on Heroku

As you can see, deploying to Heroku infrastructure is very straightforward, you
don't have to worry about the server details such as the HTTP server or the process
management so that you can focus on your application development and forget
about the infrastructure.

If you have any issues with your application in production, you can see what's
happening with the `logs` command:

```
$ heroku logs -tail
```

This will show the last log messages in the Heroku server. Please consult the online
documentation of the service for more details; here you can find information about
how to scale your application, connect Dyno instances to databases, and so on.

Production environment

If you have a bare metal server or want to work with virtual servers, such as
DigitalOcean or Rackspace, you can create your own production environment.
In this section, you will see how to make it possible.

It doesn't matter what the case is as the way you configure a production environment on these kind of servers are the same. However, keep in mind that the production environment that you will see here is for simple web applications.

If you have an application with high traffic, you can start from here; however, the server architecture should have a sophisticated organization. The details on how to scale your deployments are out of the scope of this book.

For the server, I will use the Ubuntu server as it is the easiest and the most popular choice to deploy application. If you are familiar with other distributions such as CentOS, you can use it; however, the instructions are not the same.

The following diagram shows you a typical configuration for a **Node** server in the production environment:

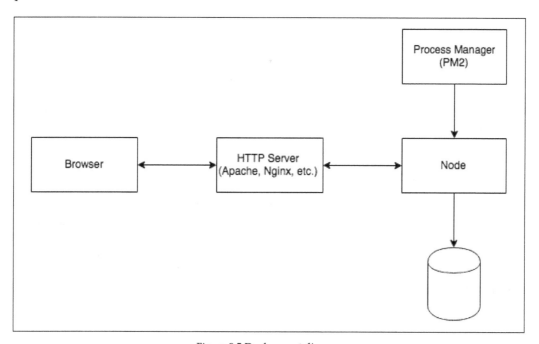

Figure 9.5 Deployment diagram

As Node was not built to be a full-featured and robust web server, you should put an HTTP server in front to answer the client requests instead of using Node directly. The HTTP server will forward the request to the Node process and return the response from the Node server to the user.

In the preceding diagram, you can see that we are using a **Process Manager**, its work is to keep the Node process up and alive; if the Node process crashes for some reason, **PM2** will take care of it and restart the process.

Also, you can monitor the memory and processor that your application is consuming in real time, manually restart and stop processes, check logs, and so on. Finally, the access to the database is made from the **Node** server.

When a user makes a request from its browser, the server will process the request as follows:

- The client sends a request to the server host
- An HTTP server takes the request
- The HTTP server forwards the request to the Node server
- The Node process makes its internal process of the request
- The Node process returns an answer to the HTTP server
- The HTTP server forwards the answer to the client
- The client receives the request

In the following sections, we will explore how to install and configure all the components in order to have a Node application running. We will use an **Ubuntu-14.04** box to perform the installation process. If you have a different environment, the configuration content should still work; however, the instructions to install and the location of the configuration files may be different.

The HTTP Server

The HTTP server handles the connections with the client and forwards all the requests to the Node server. In some way, it is a kind of proxy. Currently, there are two main HTTP servers on the market that were used widely in production: Apache and Nginx, both can be used to server Node applications. However, in this book, we will cover Nginx. The main reason for this decision is its simplicity and performance and it is smaller than Apache.

To install Nginx, use `apt-get`:

```
$ sudo apt-get install nginx
[sudo] password for abiee:
Reading package lists... Done
Building dependency tree
Reading state information... Done
The following extra packages will be installed:
  nginx-common nginx-core
Suggested packages:
```

```
  fcgiwrap nginx-doc
The following NEW packages will be installed:
  nginx nginx-common nginx-core
0 upgraded, 3 newly installed, 0 to remove and 30 not upgraded.
Need to get 348 kB of archives.
After this operation, 1297 kB of additional disk space will be used.
Do you want to continue? [Y/n] Y
```

After the Nginx server is installed, Ubuntu will start the server automatically; however, you can manage the server daemon with the service command:

```
#Start the nginx server
$ sudo service nginx start
#Stop the nginx server
$ sudo service nginx stop
#Restart the nginx server
$ sudo service nginx restart
```

You can check whether the server is running by pointing your browser to the server IP, as shown in the following screenshot:

Figure 9.6 Nginx fresh installation

The Nginx configuration files are located at /etc/nginx, in this path are two more paths, as follows:

- **sites-available**: Each file is a configuration of a single host (subdomain). Note that these files are not active until they are not in sites-enabled.

- **sites-enabled**: While the sites-available has a set of configuration files, the sites-enabled are a set of sites that are actually active.

To create a new site, you need to create a new configuration file in the sites-available path:

```
$ sudo editor /etc/nginx/sites-available/webapp
```

The configuration content is shown in the following:

```
upstream webapp {
    server 127.0.0.1:8000;
}

server {
    listen 80 default_server;

    # Configure logs
    access_log /var/log/nginx/webapp.access.log;
    error_log /var/log/nginx/webapp.error.log;

    # Make site accessible from http://www.example.com/
    # server_name localhost;
    server_name www.example.com;

    location / {
        # Proxy headers
        proxy_set_header X-Real-IP $remote_addr;
        proxy_set_header X-Forwarder-For $proxy_add_x_forwarded_for;
        proxy_set_header Host $http_host;
        proxy_set_header X-NginX-Proxy true;

        # Proxy to Nodejs
        proxy_pass http://webapp;
        proxy_redirect off;
    }
}
```

The upstream module of Nginx defines a server or a group of servers that can be referenced as `proxy_pass`, what it means is that the target to hit when a request is incoming at Nginx. Server configuration creates a new virtual host listening for requests to the `server_name` address. In this case, it is listening for www.example.com.

In the `location` block, it describes how to handle the requests; in the previous example, it will forward the request to the `webapp` upstream, which points to `127.0.0.1:8000`. To activate the site, you need to link the contents of this file to the `sites-enabled` path:

```
$ sudo ln -s /etc/nginx/sites-available/webapp /etc/nginx/sites-enabled/
```

Maybe you will need to delete the previous default-enabled site:

```
$ sudo rm /etc/nginx/sites-enabled/default
```

Then restart the Nginx server in order to load the new configuration:

```
$ sudo service nginx restart
```

If everything is OK, the server will be up:

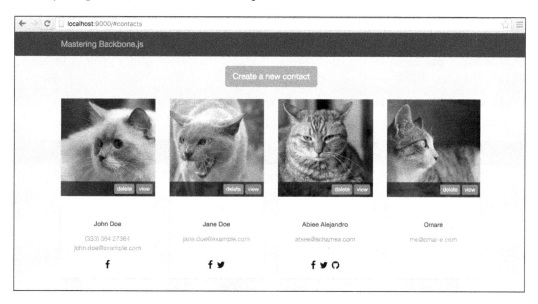

Figure 9.7 Nginx running without node.js working

The preceding image shows a `502` error, that's because the Nginx server is pointing to the `proxy_pass` setting that has the `127.0.0.1:8000` address; however, nothing is running on that socket. You need to have something listening for requests on the `127.0.0.1:8000` socket, therefore, you should run the project in the same host and the `502` error will go away:

```
$ npm install --production
$ nodejs app.js
```

This should be enough to make the server work. However, we don't want to run the `app.js` script manually each time, there is a better way to launch the node process automatically.

Do not run as root

Running the server process as root can be dangerous. If someone discovers a vulnerability in node or in your application code, then they can cause serious damage to the system. It's always a good idea to create a user to run the application server only:

```
$ sudo useradd -m production
```

The m option will create a home path located at /home/production, where you can clone the project repo:

```
$ sudo su - production
$ cd ~
$ git clone https://example.com/path/to/the/project.git
```

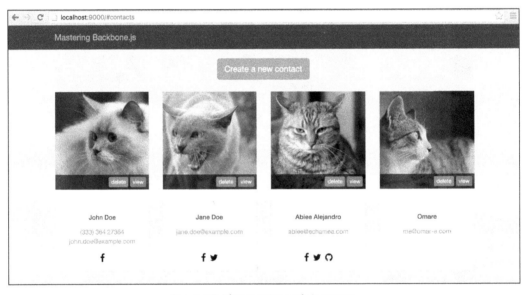

Figure 9.7 After running node.js process

Process Management

Anytime you run a program in your computer, it can fail for many reasons: maybe a server that it depends on is turned off or, even worst, an unhandled exception can tear down the running process. That's terrible for production applications as you leave your users without the server until you notice that it is not working.

This is where the process manager comes in, you can run your code behind a process manager and it will ensure that the process is always running. If something fails and crashes the program, the process manager will reset the entire application automatically.

There are two popular process managers for Node: `forever` and pm2, both work in a similar way; however, pm2 seems to be more popular and provides more utility tools than ever. For this reason, we will use pm2 for the stack.

Ubuntu comes with an integrated process manager known as Upstart. You can use the operative system process manager; however, pm2 is focused on node applications, it allows you to run more than an instance of your process instead of running a single process.

You can install pm2 with the npm tool, do not forget to install it as global package:

```
$ npm install -g pm2
```

After the installation is complete, you can run your process behind pm2 with the start command:

```
$ pm2 start app.js
[PM2] Starting app in fork_mode (1 instance)
[PM2] Done.
```

App name watching	id	mode	pid	status	restart	uptime	memory
app disabled	0	fork	16427	online	0	0s	15.801 MB

```
Use `pm2 show <id|name>` to get more details about an app
```

After you do this, the script is running and you can see the output of the process with the logs command and the application ID:

```
$ pm2 logs 0
[PM2] Tailing last 20 lines for [0] process

app-0 (out): Server running
app-0 (out): GET / 200 5.911 ms - 8908
```

```
app-0 (out): GET /css/vendor.css 200 2.740 ms - 131
app-0 (out): GET /js/app.js 200 3.821 ms - 396191
app-0 (out): GET /api/contacts 200 2.528 ms - 55
```

```
[PM2] Streaming realtime logs for [0] process
```

Instead of using the raw ID of the process, you can name your running processes:

```
$ pm2 start app.js --name app
```

You can also run more than one instance so that you can have two running instances of the same application and pm2 will load and balance requests between them:

```
$ pm2 start app.js --name app -i 2
```

It's a good idea to run more than one instance of a Node server as the Node blocks is making I/O operations. If you run more than one instance, then the other processes can continue serving the incoming requests while the other is blocked.

You can save the application parameters in a JSON file and use it instead of putting all the options in the command line:

```
{
  "apps": [{
    "name": "contacts-app",
    "script": "/path/to/the/application/app.js",
    "cwd": "/path/to/the/application",
    "watch": false,
    "instances": 2,
    "error_file": "/path/to/your/home/contacts-app/app-err.log",
    "out_file": "/path/to/your/home/app-out.log",
    "pid_file": "//path/to/your/home/app.pid"
    "env": {
      "NODE_ENV": "production"
    }
  }]
}
```

With the JSON file, you have the advantage that you don't have to remember how to run the application as the file contains all the required configurations and the same environment is easily reproducible on different hosts.

If you are fine with your settings and everything is working as you expected, the next step is to persist the pm2 process to run it as daemon each time that the server is restarted; this is always a good idea as if the server restarts for some reason such as maintenance, your processes will spawn automatically.

Fortunately, `pm2` provides an easy way to daemonize your configuration with the `startup` command for many operative systems, as follows:

```
$ pm2 startup -h

  Usage: startup [options] [platform]

  auto resurrect process at startup. [platform] = ubuntu, centos, redhat,
gentoo, systemd, darwin, amazon
$ sudo env PATH=$PATH:/usr/local/bin pm2 startup ubuntu -u production
[PM2] Generating system init script in /etc/init.d/pm2-init.sh
[PM2] Making script booting at startup...
[PM2] -ubuntu- Using the command:
     su -c "chmod +x /etc/init.d/pm2-init.sh && update-rc.d pm2-init.sh
defaults"
 System start/stop links for /etc/init.d/pm2-init.sh already exist.
[PM2] Done.
```

The first command shows the available operative systems. As the `startup` command writes on the `/etc/` path, we need to run this command as the root user and that's the reason why we are using sudo command.

To run the daemon, you need to run the following:

```
$ service pm2-init.sh start
```

However, before running this command, you will need to dump your current configuration in the daemon configuration and if you skip this step, the service will not start any process:

```
$ pm2 start process.json
$ pm2 save
[PM2] Dumping processes
```

With this command, the current configuration of `pm2` will be used every time the server restarts or you manually restart the service.

That's how you can run your node application in a production environment; run a real HTTP server and run your node processes behind it with the help of a process manager such as `pm2`.

Summary

In this chapter, we saw how to run a Node application in the Heroku platform and in a bare metal or virtual machine server with Linux. These two methods to deploy Node applications are simple; however, they are the base for more complex deployments. You can make deployments on Docker containers, for instance. With Docker, you will need to know how to install your application in a fresh Linux installation as we did, and then, manage containers as a process like Heroku does.

In this chapter, we don't see many things related to Backbone; however, if you have a Backbone application and it is backed by Node, you probably want to put your code in production. In this chapter, we have seen how to put the output of the distribution files in a production server.

10
Authentication

Most of the web applications use some kind of authorization and authentication subsystems to allow its users to access private information of the application. However, the authentication process can be tricky if you don't have a clear idea about how to implement it as Backbone does not provide a hint about how to do it.

Backbone is authentication agnostic, which means that its does not provide objects or tools to implement an authentication strategy. The advantage is that Backbone is not coupled with an authentication mechanism and the disadvantage is that you should care about it.

As Backbone was made with REST APIs in mind, you will have to deal with the authentication mechanisms that are common in that kind of APIs. That's a good reason why Backbone does not impose or provide tools in order to authenticate users.

Another thing to keep in mind is that REST APIs should be stateless, which means that they do not keep track of the requests that you previously made. What it means for you is that if you make a login request, you will expect the server to recognize you on the subsequent requests; however, in a stateless server, it will not remember you.

This may sound crazy if you have not worked with REST web services before; however, you have to authenticate each time you make a requests to the server. That's necessary and there are many available ways to do it; you should consult the API documentation in order to know the exact details of the authentication algorithm.

Despite the many options that are available, they are very similar each other with changes in just some kind of details; however, in essence, they work in a very similar way. Therefore, don't worry about the number of different ways that are available to authenticate; learn the basics and change the details.

Stateless API authentication

Authenticate against a stateless API implies that you should authenticate each time that you make a request to the server; keep in mind that a stateless server does not keep track of the previous requests. This means that each time you make a request to the server, it will process the petition as the first one.

As sessions are not stored in the server, you should put that information somewhere else. For Backbone applications, the right place to store the session data is the browser, you can use localStorage to store and retrieve the session data and JavaScript to manage the session.

HTTP Basic authentication

The simplest way to authenticate against a RESTFul API is with the HTTP Basic Authentication. The idea behind this is simple; you should include an encoded version of your username and password for every request you make. It may sound risky to send your user and password for each request, and it is. For this reason, it's highly advisable to only use Basic authentication where you have the HTTPS connections enabled:

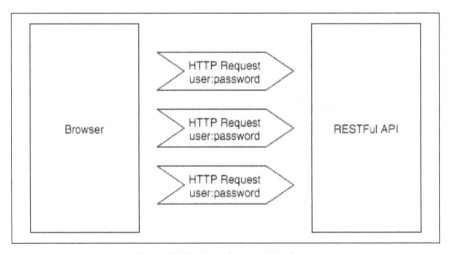

Figure 10.1 Basic authentication schema

The user and password should be sent under the Authentication header of the request. Consider the following scenario:

- User: myuser
- Password: 123456

To encode the `Authentication` header, the user and password should be concatenated with the : character as the separator.

```
myuser:123456
```

Then, the string should be encoded as `base64`, as follows:

```
$ echo myuser:123456 | base64
```

```
bXl1c2VyOjEyMzQ1Ngo=
```

The resulting string should be used for every request made to the server:

```
GET /api/contacts
Authorization: Basic bXl1c2VyOjEyMzQ1Ngo=
```

The server will decode and authenticate you for each request you make. Remember that you should not use this mechanism without HTTPS. It's very easy for someone to intercept a request header and decode the string in order to discover your user and password.

The OAuth2 authentication

The OAuth2 protocol was made to share resources among services without the use of a user and password. It is possible that you have used an application where you can authenticate using a social network account. That's OAuth2 in action. The OAuth2 authentication is an authorization framework described in RFC 6749, as follows:

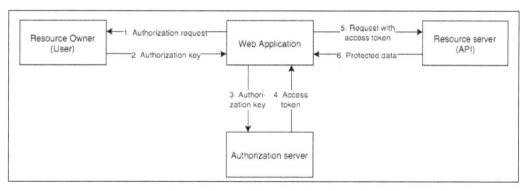

Figure 10.2 OAuth2 abstract flow

In the preceding figure, you can see an abstract diagram of authentication using the OAuth2 algorithm. You can identify the next entities, as shown in the following:

- A **Resource Owner** is the entity that owns the protected data. This is normally a person.
- The **Web application** is the application that wants to access the private data of the Resource Owner.
- An **Authorization server** identifies and authenticates the users of the Resource server, where the protected data lives.
- An **Access token** is the data to be used in the Resource server in order to authorize the resource access. The Access tokens normally have an expiration time.
- The **Resource server** is the host that serves the protected data.

Note that the Resource server and the Authorization server can be the same host. The authentication process is as follows:

1. The application asks for authorization to the resource owner.
2. The resource owner authorizes and an authorization key is issued.
3. The application uses the authorization key to exchange it for an access token.
4. The authorization server validates the authorization key and the applications.
5. The authorization server issues an access token and returns it to the application.
6. The application can use the access token to access the protected resources.

The issued access token should normally expire from time to time in order to prevent an attacker from using it maliciously. When a token expires, the application should repeat the authentication process.

However, it's not practical to log in each time that a token expires. In order to prevent this, the authorization server issues another token named `refresh token` that can be used to issue a new access token when the current access token expires.

Service applications

When you want to access the private data of a service such as Facebook, Twitter, Google, and so on, you must register your application with the service first. When you register your application with the service, they will ask you for an application name, description, website, and so on.

When the application is registered, the service will give you some tokens to identify your application, these tokens include two key data, as follows:

- **ClientID**: This univocally identifies your application against the service
- **ClientSecret**: This is used to authenticate whether the request made with a given ClientID is legitimate

If the REST server that you are building for your application is accessed only by you, you can manually generate a `ClientID` and `ClientSecret` as constant values in the application.

If your REST server will expose a public API for anyone who wants to play with the application data, you should develop some kind of application registration (such as user signup) in order to allow others to register their applications.

OAuth2 grant types

In the previous section, you have seen the OAuth2 protocol as an abstract schema of authentication. The RFC 6749 document specification describes four different ways to obtain an access token.

Authorization code grant

Authorization code grant is the most complete authorization flow; its main usage is to access private resources of the user from another server:

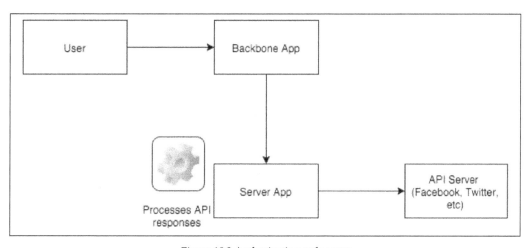

Figure 10.3 Authorization code grant

Refer to preceding figure. Server App is an application server (such as Node.js, Python, and so on), and the API Server is a third-party server, where the private resources lives (such as Facebook, Google, and so on).

In the Authorization Code Grant scenario, the Server App wants to access the data from the API Server in benefit of the **User**. This is done through the Server App; as the user interacts with Backbone App, it makes requests to the Server App, then Server App can fetch the data from the API Server, apply some processing, and return a response to the Backbone App.

The Backbone App never establishes a single connection to the API Server, it is the responsibility of Server App so that Backbone App only sees a single Server App.

Implicit Grant

This is a simplification of Authorization Code Grant; the usage of implicit grant is for pure frontend applications without server or mobile applications:

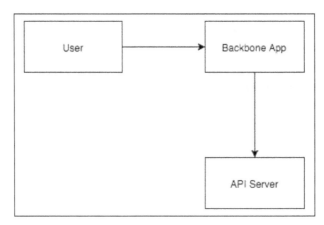

Figure 10.4 Implicit grant

In the implicit grant, App Server does not exist, therefore, the Backbone App should communicate directly with the API Server. Despite the simplicity of the implicit grant, you should be warned about the security issues.

To minimize this risk, your applications should be secured with HTTPS and do not use this flow type if you don't have it enabled. Another related issue is that this grant type does not issue a refresh token, which means that you should re-login when the access token expires.

Resource Owner Password Credentials Grant

This grant type is useful when the Backbone App and API Server are the same application. In other words, the frontend application and the backend server are developed by you, which means that you are not accessing to third-party resources.

As your application owns all the resources, you will need the user and password of the application to authenticate it:

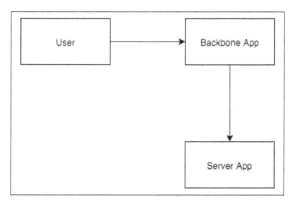

Figure 10.5 Resource owner password

The preceding diagram is very similar to the Implicit Grant diagram; however, in this case, you don't need to use ClientID and ClientSecret tokens, which simplifies the authentication process.

When you use this grant type, it feels like the classic way of authentication; you should send your user and password to the server and it will then tell you whether your credentials are valid or not. If they are valid, you will receive a valid access token that you can store and use as you want.

Client credentials grant

Client credentials grant is used when you have a trusted client that accesses the server resources. A business partner, for example. In this grant type, you are not authenticating an user but an application, therefore, you don't need an user or password.

In this grant, you should use ClientID and ClientSecret, if the API Server trusts the client, an access token will be issued.

Figure 10.6 Client credentials

Resume

In the previous sections, you have seen how to use the OAuth2 framework to authenticate against a REST server; in the OAuth2, specifications are described in four ways to make authentication and the use of any one of them depends on the requirements of the application.

However, the goal of the all these grant types is to get an access token that can be used for the next server request. Once you have an access token, the interaction with the API server should be transparent for Backbone App, the token should be send without the knowledge of rest of the application.

Implementing HTTP Basic Authentication

Let's implement the Basic Auth protocol in `Contacts App`. As you have learned in the previous sections, you will need to add the `Authorization` header for every request that you make to the server in order to be authenticated. From the server side, you will need to read and parse this header.

A useful `npm` package to decode the `Authorization` header has been developed. With the `basic-auth` module, you can read the request headers and return an object with two fields: `name` and `pass`, these fields can be used to authenticate the user. For simplicity, we will use a hardcoded user and password, not a real database:

```
// server/basicAuthMiddleware.js
var basicAuth = require('basic-auth');

var authorizationRequired = function (req, res, next) {
  var credentials = basicAuth(req) || {};

  if (credentials.name === 'john' && credentials.pass === 'doe') {
    return next();
  } else {
    return res.sendStatus(401);
  }
};

module.exports = authorizationRequired;
```

The middleware checks whether the user is `john` and the password is `doe`. If not, an HTTP `401` error will be sent to the client. You can use the middleware for each resources that you want to protect:

```
var controller = require('./controller');
var authorizationRequired = require('./basicAuthMiddleware');


module.exports = routes = function(server) {
  server.post('/api/contacts',
authorizationRequired, controller.createContact);
  server.get('/api/contacts',
authorizationRequired, controller.showContacts);
  server.get('/api/contacts/:contactId',
authorizationRequired, controller.findContactById);
  server.put('/api/contacts/:contactId',
authorizationRequired, controller.updateContact);
  server.delete('/api/contacts/:contactId',
authorizationRequired, controller.deleteContact);
  server.post('/api/contacts/:contactId/avatar',
authorizationRequired, controller.uploadAvatar);
};
```

The `WWW-Authenticate` header that we include in the HTTP 401 response will make sure that the browser prompts a dialog box asking you for a user and password. You can use the `john` user and the `doe` password in the dialog, then the browser will build and send the Authentication header for you:

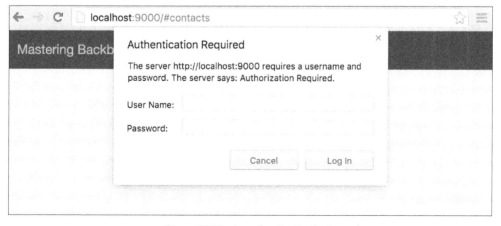

Figure 10.7 Basic authentication login

To have more control over how to ask for authentication, you can create a `form` view and add some routes for authentication purposes:

```html
<div class="col-xs-12 col-sm-offset-4 col-sm-4">
<div class="panel">
<div class="panel-body">
<h4>
Login required
</h4>
<p>
Use 'john' as user and 'doe' as password.
</p>
<form>
<div class="form-group">
<label for="username">User</label>
<input type="user" class="form-control"
  id="username" placeholder="Username">
</div>
<div class="form-group">
<label for="password">Password</label>
<input type="password" class="form-control"
  id="password" placeholder="Password">
</div>
<p id="message" class="pull-left"></p>
<button type="submit" class="btn btn-primary
pull-right">Login</button>
</form>
</div>
</div>
</div>
```

The `LoginView` method should handle the authentication process when the user clicks the **Login** button:

```js
// apps/login/views/loginView.js
'use strict';

var Common = require('../../../common');
var template = require('../templates/login.tpl');

class LoginView extends Common.ModelView {
  constructor(options) {
    super(options);
```

```
      this.template = template;
    }

    get className() {
      return 'row';
    }

    get events() {
      return {
        'click button': 'makeLogin'
      };
    }

    makeLogin(event) {
      event.preventDefault();

      var username = this.$el.find('#username').val();
      var password = this.$el.find('#password').val();

  console.log('Will login the user', username,
              'with password', password);
    }
}

module.exports = LoginView;
```

A new route should be added to show the `#/login` form:

```
// apps/login/router.js
'use strict';

var Backbone = require('backbone');
var LoginView = require('./views/loginView');

class LoginRouter extends Backbone.Router {
  constructor(options) {
    super(options);

    this.routes = {
      'login': 'showLogin'
    };

    this._bindRoutes();
```

```
    }

    showLogin() {
      var App = require('../../app');
      var login = new LoginView();

      App.mainRegion.show(login);
    }
  }

  module.exports = new LoginRouter();
```

You will need to include this new router when the application bootstraps, as follows:

```
// app.js
// ...

// Initialize all available routes
require('./apps/contacts/router');
require('./apps/login/router');

// ...
```

When an unauthenticated user accesses the `#/contacts` route, Backbone Application should redirect them to the login form:

```
Backbone.$.ajaxSetup({
  statusCode: {
    401: () =>{
      window.location.replace('/#login');

    }
  }
});
```

When the server responds with an HTTP 401, it means that the user is not authenticated and you then can show the login window. Remember to remove the `WWW-Authenticate` response header in order to prevent the browser from showing its login dialog:

```
function unauthorized(res) {
  // res.set('WWW-Authenticate', 'Basic realm=Authorization
Required');
  return res.sendStatus(401);
};
```

Figure 10.8 Login form

Now that we have a login form in place, we can put the authentication code in it. That's going to be done in the following three steps:

1. Build the Authentication string.
2. Test whether the Authentication string is valid.
3. Save the Authentication string for future requests.

The authentication string is easy to build, you can use the `btoa()` function to convert strings to `base64`, as follows:

```
class LoginView extends Common.ModelView {
  // ...

  makeLogin(event) {
    event.preventDefault();

    var username = this.$el.find('#username').val();
    var password = this.$el.find('#password').val();
    var authString = this.buildAuthString(
      username, password
    );

    console.log('Will use', authString);
```

```
    }

  buildAuthString(username, password) {
    return btoa(username + ':' + password);
  }
}
```

Then, you can use `authString` to test whether can get the contacts resource successfully. If the server answers successfully, then the user is using the right credentials:

```
class LoginView extends Common.ModelView {
  // ...

  makeLogin(event) {
    event.preventDefault();

    var username = this.$el.find('#username').val();
    var password = this.$el.find('#password').val();
    var authString = this.buildAuthString(
      username, password
    );

    Backbone.$.ajax({
      url: '/api/contacts',
      headers: {
        Authorization: 'Basic ' + authString
      },
      success: () => {
        var App = require('../../../app');
        App.router.navigate('contacts', true);
      },
      error: jqxhr => {
        if (jqxhr.status === 401) {
          this.showError('User/Password are not valid');
        } else {
          this.showError('Oops... Unknown error happens');
        }
      }
    });
  }

  buildAuthString(username, password) {
```

```
      return btoa(username + ':' + password);
   }

   showError(message) {
      this.$('#message').html(message);
   }
}
```

If the Authentication string is valid, then the user is redirected to the contact list; however, the redirection will not work as expected as the `Authorization` header in the contact list is not sent. Remember that you should send the Authorization header for every request.

You will need to save the `Authentication` string in `sessionStorage` to be used in future requests. The `sessionStorage` is similar to `localStorage`; however, in `sessionStorage`, the data will be removed when the browser is closed:

```
class LoginView extends Common.ModelView {
   // ...

   makeLogin(event) {
// ...

      Backbone.$.ajax({
         url: '/api/contacts',
         headers: {
            Authorization: 'Basic ' + authString
         },
         success: () => {
            var App = require('../../../app');
            App.saveAuth('Basic', authSting);
            App.router.navigate('contacts', true);
         },
         error: jqxhr => {
            if (jqxhr.status === 401) {
               this.showError('User/Password are not valid');
            } else {
               this.showError('Oops... Unknown error happens');
            }
         }
      });
   }

   // ...
   }
```

The App object will be responsible for storing the token:

```
// app.js
var App = {
  // ...

  // Save an authentication token
  saveAuth(type, token) {
    var authConfig = type + ':' + token;

    sessionStorage.setItem('auth', authConfig);
    this.setAuth(type, token);
  },

  // ...
}
```

After the token is saved in `sessionStorage`, you should include the `Authorization` header for every future request:

```
// app.js
var App = {
  // ...

  // Set an authorization token
  setAuth(type, token) {
    var authString = type + ' ' + token;
    this.setupAjax(authString);
  },

  // Set Authorization header for authentication
  setupAjax(authString) {
    var headers = {};

    if (authString) {
      headers = {
        Authorization: authString
      };
    }

    Backbone.$.ajaxSetup({
      statusCode: {
        401: () => {
          App.router.navigate('login', true);
        }
      },
      headers: headers
```

```
        });
    }

    // ...
}
```

When the application is bootstrapped, it should look whether there is an active session open; if so, it should use the session, as shown in the following:

```
// app.js
var App = {
start() {
    // The common place where sub-applications will be showed
    App.mainRegion = new Region({el: '#main'});

    this.initializePlugins();

    // Load authentication data
    this.initializeAuth();

    // Create a global router to enable sub-applications
    // to redirect to
    // other URLs
    App.router = new DefaultRouter();
    Backbone.history.start();
},

    // ...

    // Load authorization data from sessionStorage
    initializeAuth() {
      var authConfig = sessionStorage.getItem('auth');

      if (!authConfig) {
        return window.location.replace('/#login');
      }

      var splittedAuth = authConfig.split(':');
      var type = splittedAuth[0];
      var token = splittedAuth[1];

      this.setAuth(type, token);
    },

    // ...
}
```

The user should be able to log out. Let's add a route for the user to log out in the App router:

```js
// app.js

// General routes non sub-application dependant
class DefaultRouter extends Backbone.Router {
  constructor(options) {
    super(options);
    this.routes = {
      '': 'defaultRoute',
      'logout': 'logout'
    };
    this._bindRoutes();
  }

  // Redirect to contacts app by default
  defaultRoute() {
    this.navigate('contacts', true);
  }

  // Drop session data
  logout() {
    App.dropAuth();
    this.navigate('login', true);
  }
}
```

The session is removed when the `auth` string is removed from `sessionStorage` and the Authentication header is not sent anymore:

```js
var App = {
  // ...

  // Remove authorization token
  dropAuth() {
    sessionStorage.removeItem('auth');
    this.setupAjax(null);
  },

  // ...
}
```

That's how you can implement authorization with the HTTP Basic Auth protocol. An authorization string is generated and attached for every request made to the server, that's done with the help of the `ajaxSetup()` method of jQuery. In the following section, we will see how to implement the OAuth2 protocol.

Implementing OAuth authentication

As we did for Basic Auth, we are going to build a server-side implementation of the OAuth2 protocol. As the Backbone App and Server App are both built by us, the best grant type to choose is *Resource Owner Password Credentials Grant*.

A difference from Basic Auth is that OAuth2 needs to add an endpoint that is used to issue access and refresh tokens. As described in RFC-6749, the requests made to this endpoint should include the following:

> *The client makes a request to the token endpoint by adding the following parameters using the "application/x-www-form-urlencoded":*
>
> > *grant_type: REQUIRED. Value MUST be set to "password".*
> >
> > *username: REQUIRED. The resource owner username.*
> >
> > *Password: REQUIRED. The resource owner password.*

A valid request will look as shown in the following:

```
POST /api/oauth/token HTTP/1.1
Host: example.com
Content-Type: application/x-www-form-urlencoded

grant_type=password&username=john&password=doe
```

Then, the server will respond with a valid access token, an optional refresh token, and a token type; it could contain additional values, as follows:

```
HTTP/1.1 200 OK
Content-Type: application/json;charset=UTF-8
Cache-Control: no-store
Pragma: no-cache

{
    "access_token":"2YotnFZFEjr1zCsicMWpAA",
    "token_type":"example",
    "expires_in":3600,
    "refresh_token":"tGzv3JOkF0XG5Qx2TlKWIA",
    "example_parameter":"example_value"
}
```

The `token_type` value tells the client about the kind of token that was issued, in our case, it is `Bearer`. We can start the implementation by creating the necessary functions in order to issue authorization tokens:

```
function authorize(data, callback) {
  var grantType = data.grant_type;
  var username = data.username;
  var password = data.password;

  if (grantType !== 'password') {
    return callback({error: 'invalid_grant'});
  }

  if (!username || !password) {
    return callback({error: 'invalid_request'});
  }

  if (username === 'john' && password === 'doe') {
    issueAuthorization(username, callback);
  } else {
    callback({error: 'invalid_grant'});
  }
}
```

As specified in the RFC document, if the grant type is not supported, then we should respond with an `invalid_grant` error; and if a parameter is missing in the request, then we should respond with an `invalid_request` error.

If the username and password coincide, then we can issue an authorization token:

```
const DEFAULT_EXPIRATION_TIME = 3600; // seconds (1 hour)

// ...

function issueAuthorization(username, callback) {
  var accessToken = generateToken();
  var refreshToken = generateToken();
  var token = {
    access_token: accessToken,
    token_type: 'Bearer',
    expires_in: DEFAULT_EXPIRATION_TIME,
    refresh_token: refreshToken
  };

  saveValidToken(token, username);
  callback(token);
}
```

The generated tokens are just a random string generated with the `generateToken()` function, as follows:

```
const TOKEN_LENGTH = 20;

// ...

function generateToken() {
return crispy.base32String(TOKEN_LENGTH);
}
```

These tokens should be stored somewhere in order to be validated for future requests. For simplicity, in this book, we will store the tokens in memory objects; however, you can use a databases such as Redis for real projects:

```
var validTokens = {};
var refreshTokens = {};

// ...

function saveValidToken(token, username) {
  var tokenCopy = _.clone(token);
  tokenCopy.username = username;

  validTokens[token.access_token] = tokenCopy;
  refreshTokens[token.refresh_token] = tokenCopy;

  setTimeout(function() {
    expireToken(tokenCopy.access_token);
  }, DEFAULT_EXPIRATION_TIME * 1000);
}

function expireToken(token) {
  delete validTokens[token];
}
```

The `validTokens` and `refreshTokens`are hash tables store the tokens. The tokens in `validTokens` should be removed after the **TTL (Time to live)** expires, the `setTimeout()` call will ensure that these items are automatically removed.

To validate whether a user is authenticated, we just need to check whether the token is active in the `validTokens`hash table, as follows:

```
function authenticate(token, callback) {
  if (_.has(validTokens, token)) {
```

```
        callback({valid: true, token: validTokens[token]});
      } else {
        callback({valid: false, token: null});
      }
    }
```

With the function that is described in this section, it is possible to implement OAuth2 in our Contacts App project. Let's add a route in order to generate the access tokens and add a middleware to protect the resources, as follows:

```
var controller = require('./controller');
var auth = require('./oauth2Middleware');

module.exports = routes = function(server) {
  server.post('/api/oauth/token', auth.authenticate);
  server.post('/api/contacts', auth.requireAuthorization,
    controller.createContact);
  server.get('/api/contacts', auth.requireAuthorization,
    controller.showContacts);
  server.get('/api/contacts/:contactId',
    auth.requireAuthorization, controller.findContactById);
  server.put('/api/contacts/:contactId',
    auth.requireAuthorization, controller.updateContact);
  server.delete('/api/contacts/:contactId',
    auth.requireAuthorization, controller.deleteContact);
  server.post('/api/contacts/:contactId/avatar',
    auth.requireAuthorization, controller.uploadAvatar);
};
```

The `oauth2Middleware` module provides the `requireAuthorization()` middleware and the `authenticate()` authentication handler as described in the following:

```
module.exports = {
  authenticate(req, res) {
    authorize(req.body || {}, _.bind(res.json, res));
  }
}
```

To issue a new token, you need to call the `authorize()` function, which returns a valid OAuth2 response as specified in the RFC document:

```
requireAuthorization(req, res, next) {
  var authorization = req.headers.authorization || '';

  if (!authorization) {
```

```
      return res.sendStatus(401);
    }

    var splitValues = authorization.split(' ');
    var tokenType = splitValues[0];
    var token = splitValues[1];

    if (!tokenType || tokenType !== 'Bearer' || !token) {
      return res.sendStatus(401);
    }

    authenticate(token, function(response) {
      if (response.valid) {
        next();
      } else {
        return res.sendStatus(401);
      }
    });
  }
```

The requireAuthorization() middleware is used to protect the resources with our OAuth2 protocol implementation. The middleware splits the token in two parts: the token type and the token itself; it verifies whether the token type and its existence in the active access tokens list is valid.

In the Backbone App, we can reuse the objects that we made for the Basic Auth protocol; however, we have to make small changes. In the LoginView object, you should change the url request to /api/oauth/token and change the method to POST, as follows:

```
class LoginView extends Common.ModelView {
  // ...

  makeLogin(event) {
    event.preventDefault();

    var username = this.$el.find('#username').val();
    var password = this.$el.find('#password').val();

    Backbone.$.ajax({
      method: 'POST',
      url: '/api/oauth/token',
      data: {
        grant_type: 'password',
        username: username,
```

```
          password: password
      },
      success: response => {
        var App = require('../../../app');
        var accessToken = response.access_token;
        var tokenType = response.token_type;

        App.saveAuth(tokenType, accessToken);
        App.router.navigate('contacts', true);
      },
      error: jqxhr => {
        if (jqxhr.status === 401) {
          this.showError('User/Password are not valid');
        } else {
          this.showError('Oops... Unknown error happens');
        }
      }
    });
  }

  buildAuthenticationString(token) {
    return 'Bearer ' + token;
  }

  showError(message) {
    this.$('#message').html(message);
  }
}
```

Summary

Authentication in Backbone applications can be tricky if you don't have a clear vision of how authentication works in REST servers. As Backbone is authentication agnostic, it does not force you to use an authentication mechanism. As a developer, it's your responsibility to create one or adhere to an existing one.

In Backbone Apps, backed by stateless servers, you should move the session handling code to the browser. In the examples shown in this chapter, we used sessionStorage to store the access tokens; however, you can use another storage solution such as localStorage and indexeddb, or even cookies.

Then, we saw how to combine the theory with the practical implementation of the Basic Auth and OAuth2 protocols in Contacts App. The implementation was transparent for the rest of the application, therefore, you can switch between the implementations easily.

Index

R

regions 35, 36
require() function 88
responsibilities, Backbone objects
  Collections 6
  Models 5
  routers 6
  Views 5

S

save() operation 135
spy function 196
stateless API authentication 232
subapplication anatomy 3, 4
subapplication Façade
  testing 209, 210
subapplications based architecture 2, 3

T

task runner 162, 163
templates
  modularizing 101-104
testing tools
  about 184
  assertions libraries 184
  browser testing 184
  faking tool 184
  mocking tool 184
  module mocking 184

stress tools 184
stubbing tool 184
test coverage 184
testing libraries 184
test reports 184
test runners 184
third-party plugins
  rendering 55-58
TTL (Time to live) 251
two-way binding, model binding
  about 64-67
  references 67

U

Ubuntu-14.04 box 222
upload file
  encoding 123, 124

V

views
  working 37
views, Backbone applications
  testing 194-197
view types
  CollectionView 24, 28
  identifying 24
  layout 24, 38, 39
  ModelView 24, 25
  region 24, 35
  summarizing 41-43

Thank you for buying
Mastering Backbone.js

About Packt Publishing

Packt, pronounced 'packed', published its first book, *Mastering phpMyAdmin for Effective MySQL Management*, in April 2004, and subsequently continued to specialize in publishing highly focused books on specific technologies and solutions.

Our books and publications share the experiences of your fellow IT professionals in adapting and customizing today's systems, applications, and frameworks. Our solution-based books give you the knowledge and power to customize the software and technologies you're using to get the job done. Packt books are more specific and less general than the IT books you have seen in the past. Our unique business model allows us to bring you more focused information, giving you more of what you need to know, and less of what you don't.

Packt is a modern yet unique publishing company that focuses on producing quality, cutting-edge books for communities of developers, administrators, and newbies alike. For more information, please visit our website at www.packtpub.com.

About Packt Open Source

In 2010, Packt launched two new brands, Packt Open Source and Packt Enterprise, in order to continue its focus on specialization. This book is part of the Packt Open Source brand, home to books published on software built around open source licenses, and offering information to anybody from advanced developers to budding web designers. The Open Source brand also runs Packt's Open Source Royalty Scheme, by which Packt gives a royalty to each open source project about whose software a book is sold.

Writing for Packt

We welcome all inquiries from people who are interested in authoring. Book proposals should be sent to author@packtpub.com. If your book idea is still at an early stage and you would like to discuss it first before writing a formal book proposal, then please contact us; one of our commissioning editors will get in touch with you.

We're not just looking for published authors; if you have strong technical skills but no writing experience, our experienced editors can help you develop a writing career, or simply get some additional reward for your expertise.

Backbone.js Blueprints

ISBN: 978-1-78328-699-7   Paperback: 256 pages

Understand Backbone.js pragmatically by building seven different applications from scratch

1. Gain insights into the inner working of Backbone to leverage it better.

2. Exploit Backbone combined with the features of a Node powered server.

3. Learn how to build seven step-by-step frontend applications.

Backbone.js Cookbook

ISBN: 978-1-78216-272-8   Paperback: 282 pages

Over 80 recipes for creating outstanding web applications with Backbone.js, leveraging MVC, and REST architecture principles

1. Easy-to-follow recipes to build dynamic web applications.

2. Learn how to integrate with various frontend and mobile frameworks.

3. Synchronize data with a RESTful backend and HTML5 local storage.

4. Learn how to optimize and test Backbone applications.

Please check **www.PacktPub.com** for information on our titles

Backbone.js Essentials

ISBN: 978-1-78439-479-0   Paperback: 180 pages

Build amazing high-performance web applications using Backbone.js

1. Construct top-notch web applications by mastering the powerful tools provided by Backbone.js.

2. Gain insights into how to simplify data management and create single-page web applications with powerful user interfaces.

3. This is a fast-paced guide on how to test, document, and leverage third-party libraries, and helps you get the most out of Backbone.js.

Backbone.js Patterns and Best Practices

ISBN: 978-1-78328-357-6   Paperback: 174 pages

A one-stop guide to best practices and design patterns when building applications using Backbone.js

1. Offers solutions to common Backbone.js related problems that most developers face.

2. Shows you how to use custom widgets, plugins, and mixins to make your code reusable.

3. Describes patterns and best practices for large scale JavaScript application architecture and unit testing applications with QUnit and SinonJS frameworks.

Please check **www.PacktPub.com** for information on our titles